AF364290

*I feel humility in my heart of hearts only in the presence
of the poorest lives and the greatest adventures of the mind.
Between the two is a society I find ludicrous.*

ALBERT CAMUS

WANDER

GREGORY REWEGA

WANDER

GREGORY REWEGA

WANDER

Copyright © Gregory Rewega, 2016

1st edition.

First published 2016
Published by Mohammed Hussein Miheasen, Denmark

Cover Photo © Gregory Rewega

Cover and Book design ©
Gregory Rewega and Mohammed Massoud Morsi

ISBN 978-87-995401-7-4 [Paperback]
ISBN 978-87-995401-8-1 [Ebook]

CONTENTS

For Mum

IN
THE
COMPANY
OF
PIRATES

The pirates arrived at dinner time on a Sunday. It was a muggy, grey, windless evening and the Java Sea looked like laksa soup with whirlpools and eddies pulsating indiscriminately under its glassy top.

I was sitting in the galley with my headphones on, eating the chef's baked cod and listening to The Chemical Brothers. I found The Chemical Brothers' music perfect for a swing on an oil rig because their chaotic melodies and upbeat riffs helped to displace preoccupations and dissuade thinking about the unescapable steel island I inhabited.

It was only one pirate at first. I noticed him through the galley porthole; a lean, coffee coloured man, who ran past barefooted with a machete in his outstretched hand. He was dressed in a sleeveless shirt and ripped jeans with a bandana around his head and a cigarette clenched between his teeth. So clichéd and out of place. "Oh, there goes a pirate," I thought to myself before returning my attentions to the plate of fish. In my defence, I'd just come off shift and I was tired, but the impending implications of such a sight returned quickly to my mind, and removing my headphones I turned to the roughneck sitting alongside me.

Brett was, by his own admission, a scrapper, and he looked it too. A six foot five brute of a man who hailed from some small town on the Mississippi, he was all long bones lashed with muscle. Brett was always telling me stories about his brother, a professional cage fighter, and how he too could be a cage fighter but now, after scrapping his way through his twenties, he'd come to the conclusion he was a lover not a fighter. He'd recently had the word LOVE tattooed across one set of knuckles to attest to the decision. Both of his forearms were also covered in ink, not exactly individual designs, more the common tribal rip off patterns one sees all the time. He liked to think, with the ink and his cap on back-to-front, he was starting to look a little more like his hero, Fred Durst from Limp Bizkit.

"Brett, did you see that?" I pointed to the window.

"What man? Potsey hurling again?"

"Nooo… I think it was a pirate."

He started to laugh. "Pirate, man, in your dreams cowboy."

Then, as if on cue, two men, both attired similarly to the one on the deck with scowling faces and long machetes entered the galley pushing the Captain and the radio operator in front of them, while from the other entrance came two more, one armed with a pistol, the other an AK-47.

It was six o'clock, the end of the day, and the galley was full of men freshly showered and eating. As forks were dropped and bodies shuffled in their seats, turning to comprehend what was taking place, the pirate with the AK-47 let off a round and under the weight of the deafening noise and a falling cloud of insulation everybody's heads dropped back to their plates.

"No move! No move, no problems!"

I lifted my head from the table, slowly turned to our subjugators and discreetly removed a mash of fish from my left ear.

The one doing all the talking was shirtless, his torso lean and ripped, his face strong and square with sharp edges, like the blade on his machete, typically Javanese, while his eyes, wide and crazed, constantly flickered at an irrational pace.

"No trouble when you do as we say, but trouble, much trouble, biiggg trouble, when you don't... No move, no fucken move! OK?"

As he was speaking the remainder of the crew, ten in total with their hands on their heads, were led into the galley by two more pirates. A glance around the room showed six pirates and a collective fear invading the faces of the twenty-five rig workers held captive.

As the leader spoke he waved his machete in one hand and pushed at the Captain's shoulder with the other, and even though the Captain, a solidly built, softly spoken sixty year old from Louisiana, was nearly twice his size, he suddenly looked a lot smaller.

"This not your Captain, now I your Captain, you listen to me now, OK! No fucken problems OK!" Then he turned the Captain to face him and with a swift stroke from his sharp blade, carved a crevice across his cheek. The Captain let out a yelp and raised a shaking hand to his face, but as anger creased his brow and his mouth opened to speak the pirate lent back and sent a fast kick between his legs. The Captain crumpled and collapsed, one hand to his face, the other his crotch, into a crying heap on the vinyl floor. The pirate, not missing a beat, leant down to collect a packet of Marlborough Lite which had spilled out from the Captain's shirt.

The pirates knew what they were doing. At the sight of the violation of the innocent Captain, our leader, a few of the men, of which Brett was one and I was not, jumped out of their seats in protest. Another round of fire from the AK-47 quickly had everyone back in their places.

They had destroyed the command of the vessel. Now men who were used to being led would have to change their tack, and one got the feeling by the time the confidence for such an adjustment arrived, the pirates would be long gone.

I looked at our demoralised Captain. He suddenly looked a lot older. His peaked cap, which hardly ever left his head, had come off and a long flick of hair, usually combed across his balding scalp, was hanging down across his face. The blood from his cheek ran down his neck and seemed to be quickly congealing.

Sitting at the table across from me was a bearded seaman called Spike. Although his pose was placid, his eyes were sharp. Spike knew about pirates; he'd been working ships for 30 of his 48 years and he'd seen pirates in similar waters to these on more than one occasion.

It was Spike, only four days earlier, who had suggested,

"Oil rigs ain't usually targeted, but at seven knots an oil rig at tow is damn slow and incidents are on the rise in these damned waters. The Java Sea, South China Sea," waving his arm to the vast sultry expanse, "are now more hazardous than anywhere else. If pirates want to board this thing there'll be little we can do to stop 'em."

Spike, like Brett, was tough. He was another man whose side I was glad to be on, even though the brawn of both was somewhat subdued by the evening's disturbance.

While Spike's gaze remained straight, Brett turned to me and whispered,

"Hey Jake, I reckon we can take these punks." "What?" I murmured back.

"I think we can take 'em."

"You've got to be fucking joking Brett…" I said, too loudly, prompting the leader of the pirates to glare.

"Shut up, shut the fuck up or…"

He screamed, puffed out a cloud of smoke and swung his machete making a hacking gesture in our direction. He was smoking fast, he looked wired, I was sure he was high. It was a unanimous decision to heed his advice.

"We not stay long, we take, then we leave. No problems, OK, everybody be gooood, stay cooool…" He gave a big sadistic smile and walked over to the tubby frame of the Tool-pusher.

The Tool-pusher was from Texas and one of my least favourite men on the rig due to his loudmouthed, redneck, bigoted ways. His vocabulary was full of crass assertions and sexual connotations.

"Fuck it's hot out here, I'm sweating like a paedophile on a school bus…" and "Beat that hammer boy, beat it like you're beating a nigger off your missus…" being some of his favourite turns of phrase. However, with the coming of pirates he had become unusually silent, awkward and somewhat unbalanced.

The pirate grabbed a handful of the Tool-pusher's t-shirt and pulled it up and over his head so, inverted, it sat covering his face. The Tool-pusher let out a shriek, his knees went weak, and as his arms went to nurse his fat stomach he screamed, "Don't cut me please, please man, don't cut me, pleassse…" Then he ripped a fart, and I got the feeling he may have shat his pants as well.

"Everyone same, now!" the pirate screamed. "Everyone, the same as this, NOW!" He tapped the Tool-pushers flabby tummy with the flat of his machete.

I could see his objective, blindfolded men can't fight. Nearly everyone was wearing t-shirts and those who weren't, those wearing overalls, were quickly blindfolded with t-towels from the galley.

The worn old white t-shirt I was wearing was semi-transparent; I could kind of make out what was going on. I soon realised, while the fast jabber of Indonesian rang out loud, men were being approached individually, directed out of their seats and led from the room. Then, what seemed like a long time later, though in reality it was perhaps no more than five minutes, the same men returned.

There was a lot of mumbling, grumbling but little dissension. I could literally smell fear once our sense of sight had been removed. A smell of sweat and piss began to fill the air as any predictability to the evenings proceedings dissolved and trepidation for the unknown set in.

I'd heard stories of pirates, beforehand, stories of bloated bodies floating on sultry Asian seas. I'd heard stories of merchant seaman walking the decks of cargo vessels with wooden guns, their formidable silhouettes warding off suspicious speed boats tailing in the darkness of night, stories of oil tankers disappearing without a trace and whole crews of sailors clubbed to death like seals. Conversely, I'd also heard stories of buccaneers from Kalimantan, Sumatra, and numerous small towns on the Strait of Malacca, swinging on ropes or facing firing squads in the cholera-infested gulags of Malaysia.

When it came my turn to leave my shirt was pulled from my face and I was dragged by my shoulders to my feet. The pirate who escorted me to my cabin was young. He looked no older than twenty and unlike the strong featured Javanese, his face was round and plump. I got the feeling he would be a lot happier smiling and I sensed his demeanour soften as soon as we left the galley.

I led the young pirate to my room and as we walked down the stairs, I noticed his hand at his groin, scratching at something behind the denim of his cut-off jeans. Why he would have time to play with himself I could not think, so I decided perhaps he had another motive for doing so.

As we walked along the corridor my eyes went out to a bright red fire axe sitting in bracing on the wall. The head was heavy, on one end a large rounded blade, the other a tight pointed pick. I figured with a swift movement and a little barefaced valour I could quite easily dispose of my overseer and his comparably smaller blade. But I also realised to do so would buy me a whole lot of trouble.

When we entered my cabin I turned to the young pirate blankly, acting as though I was unsure about what he wanted me to do. He shifted uncomfortably on his feet, let his rusty knife go limp, less conspicuous in his hand, and glanced about the room. Then he looked at me and said,

"Ahhh, money, you give it to me now, ok?" It was more of a question than a demand.

Although the others may have been, this one certainly wasn't cutthroat and he was a long way from ruthless as well. I went to my locker and, keeping my back to him, quickly removed two hundred dollars and my credit card, dropping both into the sleeve of a dirty shirt. Then I turned back to him with a pseudo-honest smile and my wallet, which was now empty but for a single twenty. He quickly took the wallet then pointed at my watch, which I reluctantly unhooked and handed across.

"Sorry," he said, "but I must."

"Sure," I replied, "you're a pirate, that's what pirates do right?"

"Sorry," he said again, while one of his hands again crept down and rubbed at his crotch. What the hell's going on down there? Now I was beginning to wonder.

"How old are you?"

"Seventeen." He flashed a big smile, bad teeth. "Where you from? I mean, you're not Javanese right?"

"No, not Java, Ambon."

"Ambon? Hell, you're a long way from home."

"Yes," he replied, shuffling his feet again, his face falling to the floor. "You?"

"Australia."

"Ahhh, kangaroo." He looked up with a puppy like enthusiasm, showing his age. "One day I like to visit Australia, I like very much."

"For sure," I said, "not too many pirates down that way, I'm sure you'd make a killing." I laughed and he joined me.

"Where'd you learn to speak English?"

"Missionary school, I go five years."

"But now you don't go to school?"

"No…" His eyes went back to his feet.

"What's your name?"

"Mari, you?"

"Jake."

His eyes went around the room. Noticing a surfing magazine on the desk he walked over and picked it up. As he flicked through the pages I said,

"Why do you do this?" I gestured to his knife, again his feet started shuffling.

"I mean you don't look like a pirate."

"Oh, yes, I am!" He let the magazine fall, his grip on the knife tightened, his eyes glared… but the passion was short lived.

"Hey sure," I said calming him with my hands. "Surrre you're a pirate. But I think, perhaps, you're much more than that, huh?"

He smiled, diffidently, dipped his head, raised it again, picked up the magazine and as he resumed flicking the pages, it came,

"Ambon much trouble, lots of war and fighting, lots of trouble… My one brother, he die, my other brother," he gestured with his fingers, "he die too. My father also die, much death… Now I no longer go to school, now I must make money for my family, my sisters, my mother. My cousin say his friend have boat, connections, he make business. Now I make money and my family be happy."

"Mari, if you are caught you will be shot."

"Hah, no, I not get caught, never." He didn't hesitate; he just dismissed my suggestion with a shrug of his shoulders and a shake of his head. Then he pointed to a picture in the magazine and said,

"You do this."

"Yes," I replied, "it's a lot of fun."

"Ohhh, I like, me too one day, maybe, when I am rich. I like very much."

He put the magazine back on the desk and looked towards the head.

"I need to."

"Sure thing, go right ahead."

I waved my arm as he passed by suppressing the urge to laugh, the way he felt he could trust me, he placed his knife on the desk with little regard, and entered the bathroom and started to piss without shutting the door. I heard his stream hit the bowl and then I heard him let out a short cry, and when he was done and all zipped up, he returned to me with a tortured brow.

"You have a problem." I gestured to his crotch.

"Ahhh, nooo…"

He looked at me awkwardly, shyly, shuffling on his feet until eventually he said,

"Fire, fire when I ahhh… go, very much painful."

"Oh no, you poor bastard," I shook my head.

His feet moved faster, he suddenly looked even younger. But then I remembered Cody, my roommate, his predisposition for prostitutes and an earlier allusion he'd made to a toiletry bag full of potent medication.

The son of an oil rig manager Cody had been dragged around the world. As soon as he was old enough he had followed his father into the industry and quickly adapted to oil-drilling life, the long hours, the big money, the breaks full of booze, idle days and easy women, a taste which had dissipated little over fifteen years he'd spent working steel islands.

"The first time I had a whore I was seventeen," he'd told me. "I was assigned to a rig in East Java, stacked in Banyuwangi harbour. One night I was moseying around the back deck and noticed a couple of the locals climbing down a ladder on the port leg. I snuck across, leant across the railing, and yelled at 'em,

"Hey, where the fuck are you guys are going?'

"Virgins Cody," they replied pointing into the darkness below, "virgins!"

"I stretched a little further and there in the water was a small wooden fisherman's boat tied to the leg. Squatting on the bow was an old pimp. He was fanning himself with a fist full of rupees, chain smoking Gudang Garam and listening to music crackling out from a small transistor. Behind him was a rag of a curtain which hid a small cabin. The harbour was still, the water like glass, yet the boat was rocking, if you know what I mean, damn them chocolate thighs, she couldn't have been more than sixteen."

Cody's fondness for prostitutes was not without its physical drawbacks. He'd had the Clap more than once and chlamydia more times than he cared to remember.

"Now I don't leave home without a bag full of the best cure for STD's money can buy," he'd told me on numerous occasions.

I figured Cody wouldn't mind a selection of his pills going to a good cause, so while Mari looked confused I walked across and opened Cody's locker door. After a quick search I found what I was looking for and turned back to Mari with a couple of packets of pills.

"Listen," I said, "these will help you, help to fix the fire when you piss."

"Medicine?" His eyes went wide.

"Yes, medicine."

"Ohhhh, thank you, thank you very much."

He was over the moon. He took the pills from my hand and quickly pocketed them, then made a move as if to shake it, though at the last moment he stopped, stepped back and looked embarrassed.

"No problem Mari, you must fix your problem if you're to have a family of baby pirates one day."

He continued to smile, glanced quickly in the direction of the hallway door, then reached into his other pocket and handed me back my wallet and watch.

"You keep, I cannot take."

"Damn it Mari, you're one unconventional pirate."

We both started laughing. I was about to hand him the surfing magazine and tell him to keep it, but then I smelt the sweet smell of clove-tainted smoke and turned to find another, less than jovial, pirate standing at the door.

He glared at Mari and waved his machete in my direction, flicked a smouldering butt at my chest and started screaming. I braced myself half expecting the machete to come down on my head.

Mari, with his head downcast, submitted to the abuse and when the lecture was over and he raised his head. His smile was gone and he looked like a different person. Then the reprimanding pirate reached across, snatched the wallet and watch out of my still outstretched hand and, pointing in the direction of the hall, snarled, "Go, now!"

As I walked out he booted me in the shin, not too hard, but hard enough to hurt and I limped my way back up the stairs. Then when we entered the hall leading to the galley he stopped me, with his machete, pointed to a shark identification poster pinned to the wall, laughed, and said,

"Soon you shark food, ha, ha, ha…"

I resumed my place at the table and pulled my t-shirt back over my head. I was intimidated and I was scared, but regardless of the pirate's threat I was never made to walk the plank and the rest of the time in the company of pirates passed quickly. Brett was wrong to call me a dreamer and wrong to call me a cowboy. I was the least cowboy-like amongst a veritable saloon-on-water full of them, and even though a heist by pirates had been deemed most unlikely, it had happened.

Eventually the galley became quiet and after some time we realised the pirates had departed. Slowly we began to remove the shirts from our heads, like nervous children peeking out from beneath sheets, before mad panic descended. The alarm was raised, radio calls made, and the demoralised Captain was lead to the medic's room. Funnily enough the whole disturbance had only lasted forty-five minutes and the crew on the ship out in front towing us hadn't even realised we'd been under attack; it had been a dark night. A search of the horizon was made but the pirate's boat, undoubtedly fast, had disappeared.

The redneck Tool-pusher cleaned out his pants, dusted his pride. "Thanks be to sweet Jesus lord," I heard him say, and in no time at all he was back to loud mouthing and acting tough, "If I only I had my shotgun, them curry-munching-mother-fuckers…"

Two hours later we were joined by an Indonesian patrol boat. An officer led five heavily armed men aboard and they stayed to escort us the rest of the way to Singapore. It was a gesture of consolation and nothing more, for the damage had already been done. Everyone was shattered, everyone was feeling violated, sore and sorry for themselves, none more so than the Captain. Although he held his head high, the butterfly strips keeping his cut together soon looked ragged, pathetically curled by an encroaching beard. He and almost everyone else looked strung out, for the pirates had taken the liberty of relieving everybody of their cigarettes as well.

By the time we docked in Great Keppel Harbour talk of pirates had started to slide. There was a team of investigators waiting to speak to management, and the ageing Chinese pilot, with a wispy goatee beard, who oversaw the docking of the vessel told me,

"It is very sad and most scary for you, but the trouble may get worse. If terrorists join the pirates, if terrorists steal a super tanker, a liquefied natural gas tanker, then they have a bomb, a big bomb, then there is no telling what damage they can do…"

After the gangplank was lowered there was not one roughneck who wasn't itching to get off. Thoughts of pirates were instead firmly redirected towards the replenishing of cigarettes, a thirst for beer, and a hotel on Orchard Road which Cody referred to as "Four Floors of Whores."

It was a Monday night, but it made no difference; the bars were stacked, packed. There were ladies from Thailand, ladies from the Philippines and ladies who weren't really ladies at all.

I stole away. I spent the rest of the night on my lonesome wandering the backstreets of the city's China Town. I found a cheap hotel with a terrace overlooking a lamp lit outdoor restaurant. I drank Tiger beer, I ate char kway teow and black pepper crab, and as the tropical breeze flicked at washing drying on balcony strung lines, I began to feel a little tired, then, exhausted…

In the morning I awoke to the smell of spice and green tea floating on the ever present tropical trade wind. I raised myself and left the hotel for Singapore's Botanical Gardens, where I marvelled at a multitude of orchids. Then later, as I thought of my work companions waking with sore heads and crusty reminders of the night gone, I also thought of Mari, the young pirate, the most unconventional of pirates. I mentally wished him good luck for his haphazard vocation as I lazed upon the lushest layer of grass I could find, under the shade of a mammoth Banyan tree, and I was happy as my eyelids dropped and I started to doze, because there was not one ounce of steel in sight.

DRINKING
WITH
THE
SIBERIANS

He had a way with snoring, it was insidious. Something about his manner and his frail physicality just did not measure up to the demon rumblings he emitted from his nasals as he slept. It was the last leg of the journey from Irkutsk to Moscow, and it was to take four days.

I was sharing a cabin with a couple of good old boys from New York. They were in their seventies, long-time buddies reinventing the notion of adventure, but boy could Bill snore. Sanne was from Finland, and she had been assigned the bunk opposite mine. She was having a hard time dealing with it all. Earplugs are useless against the onslaught and after the second night she bribed the guards for a berth in another cabin.

I, however, was not so fazed. I resigned myself to catching pockets of sleep during the day and in the evenings, the times when Bill and Graham sat at the foldaway table playing cards and analysing all which flashed past the window:

"Geez would ya check out the girth on that cedar, Bill."

"Surrrre, though it ain't no American oak Graaaa...."

I spent the snoring hours reading Gogol's 'Diary of a Madman' in the corridor that connected the cabin to the rest of the train. Timber towns and cedar forests flew past silhouetted by the light of a full moon.

There were two young Russian guards assigned to the carriage, each worked a twelve hour shift. They moaned to me that their jobs were in peril because their supervisor hated them. On request I wrote a letter saying what a hardworking asset they both were; I neglected to mention that they actually spent their shifts drinking tea and gambling. In return for the correspondence I was given pride of place at their tea parties. I won a stack of company issue badges, but lost most of my roubles.

It was early in the third morning, after five, when the Siberians got to me. I was walking past their cabin when one just reached out and pulled me in. They were big, burly, bearded and extremely drunk, though drunk in an established way with an ability to function regardless. They obviously knew how to drink.

They forced me to sit down between them. I surveyed the scene. Empty vodka bottles littered the floor, a full one sat on the table. Alongside, laid out on crumpled butcher's paper, was a bat sized stick of salami and a block of pungent cheese.

"What's your name?" roared one of the Siberians.

"Jacob," I reply timidly.

"Jacob, you must drink!"

He ripped the top off a new bottle, poured out half a tumbler and pushed it my way, then he filled his own glass and that of his pickled compatriot.

"Nazdorovye," he said.

"Nazdorovye," I replied meekly.

Escape seemed impossible; the door had been bolted shut. I felt their gorilla like arms at rest on my shoulders and decided to comply.

Their English was bad but my Russian was non-existent. They encouraged me to drink with gesturing hands, pouting greasy lips and wide glassy eyes. No sooner was my glass empty than it was filled again. The Siberians used a rusting bayonet to stab at slices of the salami and cheese, waving both towards my mouth. I fended off their attempts with my glass.

More vodka was produced and opened, cheap Mongolian vodka sealed with a rip top, like beer bottles of old, once opened never closed. Soon we were all laughing. The Siberians begin singing. I mumbled The Beatles' 'Here Comes the Sun,' drunk, carefree, out of tune. I snuck out when they began to get emotional, when they begin crying like a couple of caged bears. I stumbled back to my cabin. It was after nine.

Sanne was removing her earplugs. Bill had snored his last notes for the night. I slurred a good morning and clambered up onto my bunk. A valley rolled by the window, framed, in my sorry head, as a colour-filled blur, brushed by my disposition and the morning sunlight. Later they told me I was snoring, loudly! Although I cannot recall if this was so.

THE
DAY
OF
THE
DEAD

Uncanny perhaps, but it is October 29; the first day of the celebration known as Dia de los Muertos, The Day of the Dead, and in Mexico there are memorials to the dead everywhere. Streets are lined with them, from simple crosses, two sticks tied with twine, to elaborate shrines build out of concrete, topped with slate headstones or mosaic pictorials of the deceased.

"Very good for reminding you about the impermanence of life. You're alive now, but on roads like these it is not to be taken for granted," says my friend Max the Life Guard, as we leave the nameless point break where we have camped for the night.

The sun is just beginning to rise, throwing light across a barren rostrum, boulders and succulents as far as the eye can see.

We are soon back on Highway 1 cruising south, Max behind the wheel. He seems to be doing ok. Neither of us has mentioned Lena. Over the past two days so much has been said, and thoughts of Lena's demise are now as much a smudge on my mind as they are on his. We've gone as far as we can go with speculations on Lena, there's no point, she's dead. All we can do is push on to Punta Conejo and hope there's a few answers waiting for us when we arrive, answers to the many questions we've both raised, answers that even I am beginning to crave.

We stop for a taco lunch in Rosario. The sun is half way home, sitting straight and high above, bearing down. It's hot.

Dogs laze in the shade, mangy dogs, dogs that no one cares to love or own. An old lady makes our lunch and potters around preparing a feast for the dead. Caramelised pumpkins and candy skeletons sit atop a table, cooling beneath fly-wire, offerings to loved ones departed and the lady of the dead who presides over the event, the Aztec goddess Mictecacihuati.

The chilli in the tortillas bites at our throats, makes us sweat. We laugh as involuntary tears flow, then drown the fire with large cups of icy horchata.

"How you hanging in there, Max?"

"What the chilli?" he laughs.

"No, Lena."

"Hmmm, you know, all sorts of thoughts, crazy thoughts, come and go. I've been beating myself up a little bit too, going over what we once had, how it all ended, how we might have done things differently."

"You can't do that, you can't beat yourself up. You couldn't have predicted any of it, the madness of it all…"

"Yeah, I know, but besides all that I was really looking forward to seeing her again, you know? The last time we saw each other it was optimistic, it felt like old times, I just got to feeling that perhaps there was still some hope for us."

"It's a prick of a thing,"

"Yeah… anyway, it's the not knowing, that's the worst thing. It would be easy enough to believe she just drowned, I mean people drown every day, even though she was a great swimmer. I know great swimmers drown too, it's just… I've got this crazy feeling it wasn't as simple as all that."

"What do you mean?"

"Oh I don't know, and I hate to think about it really. It's just a gut feeling, you know, something from deep within. I don't know, but I need to, whatever happened to her, I need to know about it. Punta Conejo is two days driving from here Jake. I figure we'll know the truth, or be able to find out something, soon enough. It just seems so poignant today, for the days to come, the Days of the Dead and all. I just can't get her out of my head."

The highway turns east and all habitation drops away. We follow it and are soon deep into the desert which separates the west coast from the Gulf of California and the Bay of Conception; it cuts across like a black snake slithering across a stretch of beach. Cowboy dreams fill my head as cactus, tall as trees, and boulders, like the Coyote throws, dot the landscape as far as the eye can see.

Lunch has made me tired. The desert air is hot, dry, and it wraps around my face like a woollen blanket, lulling me into sleepy submission. Max drives with one arm on the wheel, the other bent, resting on the open window. The Smashing Pumpkins' 'Mellon Collie and Infinite Sadness' plays out from the stereo, he sings along. The music joins the wind, the sounds dance around my head. I feel heavy, my eyelids drop, I open them wide and laugh and laugh out loud.

"What's so funny?" he asks.

"I'm so sleepy I thought I was dreaming, but I'm still awake, it's real." I gesture to the landscape, the desolate tracts.

"Why don't you climb over the back and crash for a while?"

"No, I'm enjoying all this. It seems so pure."

"Yeah, just like a Road-Runner cartoon."

The road climbs up to a crest, then, as Max negotiates the turn at the top, a large semitrailer comes speeding over the ridge in the opposite direction. Its trailer sways awkwardly, the driver flashes its headlights wildly. It's a big rig, a black cab, its tinted windows reflect the sun like blinkers on a galloping horse of doom. Max steps on the brake and quickly pulls the van across to the side of the road until the speeding truck has passed.

"Fucking maniac!" he screams out the window, then turns to me laughing. "This highway is a runway Jake, if you flap your motorised wings hard enough it might be possible to fly."

I turn and watch the truck disappear through the rear window, just a square block quickly growing smaller on a long line of asphalt.

"Oh no, Jake, oh shit, no, no…" I turn back to Max. He has negotiated the twist at the top of the hill and we are driving down the other side.

"That's why he was flashing his lights."

"What are you talking about?"

"There." Max slows the van and points to a disturbance in the continuity of the undulating land two hundred metres up ahead.

There is a cloud of dust and a wreck of cars, two cars, the remains of a head-on, thrown from the runway into the scrub, onto a sandstone stage by the side of the road. The contents of each, vinyl and rubber, metal and life has been splashed out across the landscape, the road, as though dropped from up above. Max pulls the van across to the other side of the road, brings it to a stop and slides the gear to park.

There's a small girl standing opposite, by the verge. She is young, can't be more than five or six, and she's covered from head to toe in blood. She doesn't say anything, or do anything, she just stands there staring at us, her arms by her side, her palms facing out.

I raise a hand to my mouth.

"Oh fuck."

I look at Max, his sunglasses have gone and he's already staring at me. We hold the pose, we don't budge. Each wanting the other to make the first move, each of us wondering, is this really happening? Each secretly wishing it wasn't, wishing that like the speeding truck we could just ignore it all and be on our way.

The girl continues to stare. Bellows of pain echo out from one of the cars, a crumpled hatchback, on a small incline ten metres back from the road.

"Whadda-we-do?" I say quickly.

"Ahhhh… Look we're miles from anywhere, the nearest town is…"

Max waves a flippant hand over his shoulder.

"We've got to do something, I'll… Hell I don't know, we've got to do some- thing, ok."

He opens his door, jumps out of the van, runs around to the side door and pulls the first aid kit from beneath the bed in the back.

"Come on Jake, we've got to do this," he yells at me decisively.

I am reluctant, I am scared. It is the fear of someone else's pain, of seeing the broken, bleeding, disfigured, and of seeing the dead.

"Come on Jake!"

The call of pain continues to come from the hatchback, low, deep, morose, like a cow giving birth.

I open the door, place one foot slowly out onto the road, as though testing the temperature of the water in a bath, so reluctant to jump in head first. A sharp pain eats at my bare foot; there is glass everywhere. I pull the shard from my toe, slip my feet into my huaraches, breathe a deep breath then head out across the road with a little more determination.

There's a smell of burnt rubber and spilt gasoline and it hangs everywhere like a low lying cloud. I feel the sun through my t-shirt on my back, and in my veins, adrenaline. In stark comparison to the scene in front, I feel so very alive.

Max crouches beside the young girl. He wipes the blood from her face with his t-shirt and the hair from her eyes with his hand. She does not say anything. She just stands there staring, raises a thumb and places it in her mouth.

"She's not hurt," he says. "At least, not that I can see anyway, she looks to be ok. The blood must have come from someone else."

"Perhaps one of them?"

I point to the battered hatchback, from which groans of pain continue to come. There's a gangly man with cropped hair turning slow circles in the dirt, his arms wrapped around a small package with clothed limbs, limbs like those on a ragged doll. He shakes his head, rocks the package back and forth and kicks at the scrub with his feet.

"Hmmmm, yeah, I think so." Max reluctantly walks toward the hatchback.

I turn and look in the opposite direction, at the other car, a small utility, upside down, thirty metres away. There is one man standing alongside the wreck and the shape of a body lying in bushes nearby.

"Ok," I say, unenthusiastically, and to myself. "I'll go and see about them."

I go first to the body which is male and face down in the dirt. I crouch. I am disinclined to roll him over. He wears a checked shirt which is soaked in blood. There is a strong smell of alcohol, a smell of excrement and his head looks out of shape, a lot bigger than it should be. I don't want to see his face. Instead I check his pulse. There is none. His neck is still warm, but he is dead.

The man standing is talking gibberish. As I approach him he wanders away from me, out onto the road and starts sweeping at broken glass with his sandaled feet. The glass is fragmented windscreen though it is also broken beer bottle and tequila bottle as well, the cheap label still intact.

"Senòr," I say. "Please get off the road Senòr, come and sit down."

My Spanish is rudimentary, though he takes no notice anyway.

"Senòr."

He is a small man, small, lean, old. I place a hand on his shoulder and turn him to face me.

He wears a peaked trucker's cap, he has a bushy moustache. In between both is a wide laceration which has split his forehead in two. A river of blood is slowly running down his nose and dripping from his chin. His eyes are cloudy and miles away. He is in shock, but he is also very drunk. I feel the breath he breathes could ignite just as easily as the gasoline which seeps from the ruptured tank of his small pickup. He turns back towards the verge and as he does so, I notice he is also missing an ear, it is cut clean off.

I want to be sick. I hold my hand to my mouth, but although I retch nothing comes out. I continue to follow the man around like a useless, hapless puppy, barking at him to sit down, barking words he cannot understand.

He goes back to the utility, falls to his knees and clambers inside its twisted frame. He stretches out on the upturned roof, cradles his head and continues to mumble. On the ground nearby are some broken wooden lobster pots and a dented fibreglass icebox. The lid is gone, its contents, iced crabs, lay smashed and stuck in the dirt, broken claws, surreal gesticulations. I bend down and shake his leg.

"Senòr, please come out, let me fix your head." Though he isn't listening, he has stopped his mumbling. He is either asleep, passed out or perhaps…

Who the hell am I trying to kid? Fucking dumb, drunken bastard, I mumble to myself. It's too obvious how this calamity came about.

I place one hand on the frame in order to pull myself up and feel something soft and squishy between my fingers; it is the missing ear. I jerk my hand, throw it back, but the appendage comes with it, stuck between my fingers. I shake my hand, I flick it away and it lands nearby, speared by the spikes of a small cactus.

I stand up shivering. Should it be retrieved? Is this drunken fisherman going to live, or is he already dead? Will the surgeon they assign to attend to his injuries have the time, expertise and consideration to stitch it back on? Will he see a surgeon at all? Not likely, not anywhere near here… The ear will stay where it is and the man will have to wait for fate. I head across to help Max.

Where are all the other cars on this crazy highway? How long have we been here? Why must we do this alone? Why must I be a part of it? Lena's death and now this.

The little girl is nowhere to be seen and though the man still cradles the lifeless raggedy bundle he is no longer standing. He has slumped down cross legged onto the ground by the side of the wreck and he is weeping. I approach him, open my mouth, but nothing comes out. What I can offer him, I don't know. I notice the child in his arms is a boy and though most of the boy is broken, his face is serene, as though sleeping.

The top half of Max is bent and buried in the back of the crumpled hatchback. I slowly walk over towards him, I am so unwilling, I've seen enough for one day. The bellowing woman's voice has lost its vigour, its strength has diminished and there is only the occasional gurgling guttural groan.

From ten feet back, the interior of the car looks dark and ominous. There are two people inside.

"How you doing, mate? Can I… What can I do?" Max removes his frame from the car, his shirt and arms are covered in blood, his face is white.

"Ahhh, nothing much really Jake. I'm just trying to stem the flow of blood from a large hole at her shoulder, putting some pressure down, but she's beginning to fade. She doesn't look so good."

Blood drips from his finger as he points into the car.

"The other lady is gone, she was dead before I got here. How about them?" He gestures with his head to the utility.

"A couple of drunken fishermen, they both stink of beer and tequila. One of them is dead and the other one, well he doesn't look so good either…"

I mentally chastise myself for my unintended pun, but then the sound of an approaching car distracts me and makes us both turn around.

A Jeep towing a caravan pulls up alongside our van and the occupants, a middle-aged couple, jump out. They stand across the road for a few moments taking it all in, the confusion, the apprehension on their faces shines out like a beacon. After spotting us they come straight across and the woman says, "I'm a medic, what's the situation?"

I look at the young man still slumped on the ground nursing his dead boy.

"Carnage."

She moves past me and over to Max. Another car arrives, a family of Mexicans, and then another, a policeman in a battered dodge, looks just like The Blues Brothers.

Max moves out of the medic's way and over to me. I remove my t-shirt so he can take it and wipe the blood from his arms and neck. The policeman, who is short and fat, tilts his hat back and runs around between the cars sizing things up. His hand holds his gun as he runs, and the tails of his shirt come out as his paunch flops about.

The family of Mexicans crowd around the hatchback. In a surreal twist of fate they are related to its occupants, there is a lot of moaning and crying. An old lady bends down and pulls the young man's head to her breast.

Another man approaches the fishermen. He walks around with his hands on his hips shaking his head. Taking stock of things he stops, bends down, picks up an unbroken beer bottle, then dashes it against the road. He walks over to the upturned utility, starts swearing and then kicking, violently, at the body of the earless man inside. Another car stops, and another, all are Mexican. As one car door opens a large bunch of marigolds falls out onto the road. Golden petals fly in the desert wind.

I feel like I could just dissolve. Like I could just lie down in the dirt and melt away, have all my life sucked up into the surrounding succulents. Have all my life wrapped up and protected behind spiky hides. It is the first day of the Day of the Dead and I find it difficult to see the continuity of life, for I am surrounded by death.

Max and I wander back to the van. I pull a large container of water from inside and we wash. In the heat the blood has dried and needs to be scrubbed. As I climb back into my seat I notice blood still remains beneath my fingernails.

"Let's get out of here," says Max, "there's not a lot left for us to do. I'm sure the cop has radioed for an ambulance or something."

"I wonder where the small girl went," I say, aimlessly, still looking at my nails.

"She's probably hiding, somewhere?" he says unconvincingly.

"Anyway, I've had enough, let's go."

Five minutes pass; neither of us says a word. We just sit, stare, breathe. The policeman and some of the Mexicans lift the lady out of the hatchback and start carrying her to the policeman's car. The medic holds the lady's wrist and head. Eventually Max starts the engine and moves the van back out onto the highway and slowly up to speed. Nobody notices us leave.

"Welcome to Mexico," he says turning to me with an ironic smile.

Two days further south we look out upon a stretch of ocean which, two weeks previous, rolled thick and strong, up and down, and drowned a girl named Lena, Max's ex-girlfriend, before spitting her body back, two days later, onto a deserted beach. It's November 2nd, the Day of the Dead proper, and in towns north and south of here caramelised pumpkins and candy skeletons are being placed atop graves in celebration of the dead.

CARDBOARD WALLS

I flew to San Jose from Havana. I had cigar smoke in my hair and salsa in my gait. There were three days to wait until my next flight and my finances were dwindling. I asked the taxi driver to take me to a cheap hotel. He drove me to the 'Grand Imperial'; the joke was in the name.

The front desk was closeted in thick bulletproof glass. The attendant sat inside, beads of sweat hung from his brow. There was a small hole through which he passed door keys and collected cash, all rooms had to be paid for in advance. A sign behind the booth read: 'CAUTION: After dark you have a good chance of being robbed in the streets outside this hotel!'

The hotel was open plan, like a warehouse, filled full of small plywood rooms, stacked one beside the other, row upon row.

Each had the same décor, brown bed with old cream sheets. My bed sagged, so much so I seemed to touch the floor. But at least, I was happy to find, the sheets seemed bug free.

A dumpy lady with a black moustache swept the hallway every

morning, a cigarette hung from her hairy lip.

It wasn't so bad, the hotel had its good points. There was a restaurant attached to the side with a secure balcony overlooked the bustling street below. When darkness fell I bought a huge plate of fish fillet, salad, rice and beans for three dollars, and ate my dinner as the local drug dealers yelled and whistled at me from across the street.

"Hey there Gringo, you wanna some motor? Some cocaina? Come see, come seeee…"

In the light of day I found a maze-like market across the road, an assortment of stalls, selling all manner of goods. A couple of cafes served breakfast. I sat in a small red vinyl booth, served by a sedate lady with a falling perm who wore a blood stained apron. The percolated coffee was thick, robust and good and the waitress poured it fast, from a huge stainless steel brewing pot. A roasting machine turned nearby sending the rich smell of Costa Rican coffee throughout the whole market.

A fruit vendor took a particular interest in my wellbeing. He was a small man in a big cowboy hat who sold an array of tropical fruits from a cart parked out the front of the market. He greeted me with a big smile, bejewelled with one gold tooth shining. His concerns were for the way I carried my day pack, this he continuously brought to my attention.

"Nuevea noche."

After 9pm, he said, making a guttural noise and a throat slitting gesture with his finger.

"They will rob you blind…"

He sold the sweetest tasting bananas.

My last night at the Grand Imperial yielded little sleep. I was continuously disrupted by noise seeping in from all around the cardboard thin walls. There was loud snoring coming from one direction, the sounds of lovemaking from another. Around midnight my surfboard, perched in a narrow corner of the room, fell over knocking me on the head. Then to top things off, at five o'clock I was awoken by the sound of someone in the neighbouring shower block dying, or so it seemed, vomiting, coughing, and spluttering with all the vigour of a howler monkey.

I stuck my head out the door and implored the noise to be quiet. The bathroom door swung open and a Hispanic midget in a tuxedo fell out. He had pieces of sick dripping from his shirt and was nursing a bottle close to his chest. "Perdon Senòr," he said, "Tu gusta tequila?" He waved the bottle towards my head. I quickly shut and bolted my door.

I left the Grand Imperial soon after, choosing the airport lounge over the cardboard walls for my last hours in the Costa Rican capital. The streets were suspiciously quiet. The taxi driver drove like a madman.

ROAD
KILL

Big Red was a bad man. There was nothing good about him. Nothing I could see anyway and I tried, yes, I'm quite certain I gave it a good shot. 'They always come good,' my mother use to say. 'Everybody has some redeeming characteristics.' But Red, he just proved me wrong, every time, even when I thought he might be just about to prove me right.

We first met in the lay-down yard.

"We gotta move all of them drill pipe onto the tray of that truck. We ain't going nowhere until we do and I'm not doing it on me own, so ya better not have glass arms."

Big Red was big, solid big, big boned. He had a pale complexion, really pale, almost white, I'd say albino but I'd never have said that to Red. His limbs were like tree trunks shot with paint balls, splattered with red freckles. He kept the hair on his head short, crew cut, though it was the hair that grew on his face which really set him apart. It was his beard which gave him the name; one long, tangled crimson mass, as thick as copper wire, which stretched all the way down from his nose to his chest.

It was a solid trophy of facial hair, a McCubbin's model, a bikie's dream, a captain's legacy born of months at sea.

Red had modelled it on Ned Kelly, Kelly was his hero. He was always talking about Kelly. I don't think Red knew how to write to save himself but he'd read everything that had ever been written about Ned Kelly. It was a beautiful beard. If he was to have a redeeming feature, it was the beard, he looked as though he had been born with it. I could never imagine him without it.

Being the new, younger guy on the crew I had plenty to prove so I avoided Red's remark and walked my way down to the other end of the pile of steal drill pipe. When his aversion to the heavy lifting had passed, Red proved he had some brawn to match his steely front and we set about getting the job done. All up it must have weighed five ton. He cursed the whole way through though, sweating profusely and stopping to smoke hand rolled Capstan Blue.

At lunchtime we both bought a Coffee Chill and a Mrs Mac's. "Not a bad dogs-eyes, eh?" he said, and I agreed, but the conversation never went further than that.

By early afternoon we'd finished loading the truck. I was exhausted and as I swiped the sweat from my forehead I looked at Red with a sense of accomplishment and said, "Well looks as though we're ready to hit the road tomorrow, huh?"

But he just grunted in reply, walked over to an old model Ford and left me in a shower of dust.

I arrived early the next morning. The driller, 'Boofhead', wanted us all on the road by six. An overtly protruding forehead was the reason for his nickname, a shining mound of skin that stood out like a billboard advertising his receding hairline. One time, a few weeks later, when he was drunk, he would tell me how he had acquired the moniker early and it had stuck, as soubriquets have a tendency to do. He never seemed to care too much about it, at least he knew better than to show he did anyway. I just called him by his christian name, Ralph, I wasn't in a position to call him anything else, although his head did remind me a little of somebody out of Star Trek.

As I gave my mother a hug goodbye and thanked her for the ride, a lady who remained a shadow behind the wheel of the old Ford delivered Red, who waltzed over to us rolling a ciggie. He was wearing his signature Redwing boots, footy shorts and a long-tailed Bluey top.

"Hoz ya going, Boof?" he said, before turning to me to quip,

"Hey mummy's boy, me missus thinks you look like a weasel!"

He said it with a loud Haruff, a Hee-Hee, Haw-Haw, looking at Boofhead the whole time; just to make sure he'd heard, waiting for a response, an acknowledgement, not satisfied until Boofhead obliged him with a smile.

That was my introduction to the duplicitous side of Red. Over the following months I would get to know it well. Whenever an audience presented the opportunity he was always quick to give it a shot. I guess a psychiatrist might suggest such a performance originated from harboured insecurities, I mean, the beard would probably help to endorse such a suggestion, but I don't know about that. I just put it down to him being bad. Bad and I mean nasty, to his very core.

Whether or not Red and his lady saw me as some sort of rodent, from that day on it seemed I was destined to become an outsider. It wasn't the work that set me apart. I was as good as any other when it came to the work. It was the hours after work, when I was looking for a little innovative escape from the monotonous pace of those tiresome working days, and those long, lonesome nights.

Boofhead made towards the Land Cruiser and Red quickly followed, a stab from one of his fat fingers pointing me in the direction of the old truck.

It was a long drive. I drove all day and the truck, the old flatbed, loaded heavy with all the drill pipe, shook me to my bones. It had a temperamental gearbox and a corroded and collapsing exhaust. The engine screamed into every hill, red dust swirled out from the manifold and diesel fumes seeped up through rusted holes in the floor. I fitted earplugs to beat the racket and held my head outside the window to avoid the fumes.

By the time I arrived at the gold mining town the day was gone, evening had passed and night had descended. I found the cheap motel where we were booked for the night and then I found Boofhead and Red, perched at the bar drinking beer and throwing coins at a skimpily clad barmaid. By the look of their eyes, bleary and amber-hued, they had obviously been at it for some time.

"'Bout time you got 'ere," said Red, only I didn't quite hear it, the forgotten earplugs still embedded in my ears. "Pull out the plugs, ya fucking goose," he yelled, rousing a reception from all in the bar.

They sat there for the rest of the night. I joined them for a counter meal, but dragged my tired body away soon after. They were certainly drunk when they fell to their beds sometime after midnight; Red was snoring like a gorilla.

The next morning, after we'd bought six weeks' worth of food supplies, Boofhead drove to a liquor store and he and Red filled every spare space on the back of the ute with cartons of beer.

When I told them I was going 'dry' they both looked at me like I was truly mad, and Red said,

"Well don't think you will be getting any of mine when you change ya mind and get thirsty in a few days' time."

Leaving the town we headed north. The lonesome highway turned to a rutted track lined by desert patched scrub, then it became not much of a track at all and after driving for four hours a steal derrick came into view, towering through the trees. On rendezvousing with the exploration rig our swing began, a month and a half of twelve to thirteen hour days.

We lived out of an old caravan, but slept in swags on camp beds laid out beneath star-studded skies. Every day Red and I would run around like mad men, pushing and pulling at steel, while Boofhead screamed out orders and manhandled levers which sent the drill-string deep into virgin ground.

"Searching for the exceptions," said the resident geologist, who spent his day saying little else, lazing in his Land Cruiser and looking equally too good for us, and way too scared to get too close to the likes of us.

"Exceptions in the topography, looking for pockets of profit."

At the end of each shift, when the big diesel engine of the rig was wound down, an eerie silence descended on my world, an echo filled hush, followed by the true sounds of nature, fighting to be restored in my motor-meddled mind. But only in the fresh dawn of morning would I appreciate the birds' call, for we wasted no time in piling into the ute and pushing it through the scrub, trying to find a quicker way, each day, back to camp, so Boofhead and Red could get back to the oil, grease, and food stained fridge, the icy safe which held their precious nectar.

The days were hot, damn stinking at times. It was not uncommon for the temperature to rise above 40 degrees and next to the rig's roaring motor it always seemed 10 degrees hotter.

Each evening the three of us would take turns to cook dinner in the mould infested kitchen of the derelict caravan. Over six weeks Boofhead and Big Red concentrated on perfecting two dishes: sausages and mash, and steak and mash. They got pretty good at them too, but when it came my turn to cook, with fear of scurvy descending on the camp, I decided to spice things up a bit.

I employed all available fruits and vegetables and made a salad to accompany the main dish every night. Therefore the spaghetti bolognese would sit alongside a lightly oiled collection of lettuce, tomato, basil. The lamb vindaloo would be joined by a yoghurt, cucumber raita and the oven roasted apricot chicken would be complemented by a tabbouleh. My endeavours received a mixed response from Big Red.

"Hey this ain't too bad. What ya call it again, spaghetti bog eh?"

He'd say with a modicum of sincerity, which quickly dissolved as he tossed a piece of lettuce over his shoulder and added,

"But ya can stick ya fucking rabbit food!"

I was never destined to fit in. It could have had something to do with the carrot sticks I ate with my lunch every day, or because I preferred porridge to a cold tin of braised steak and onions in the morning.

Or perhaps it had something to do with the campfire episodes in the evening. Boofhead and Red would sit around chain-smoking, drinking beer, discussing drilling and throwing their empty cans into the fire. I would sit alongside, sipping a cup of tea, imploring them to place their empties in a rubbish bag and occasionally try to instigate a different discussion.

Where Red and Boofhead would get excited about the amount of metres a diamond rig had drilled in one day up around Wiluna way, while I'd passionately expound the possibility of low lying Pacific Islands disappearing as a direct result of global warming. Or when they started to discuss the capabilities of the latest reverse circulation air compressor, I'd try to talk about Banjo's poetry, Lawson's short stories or Patrick White's sombre grace.

The response I usually received was a blank stare and a shake of a head. I couldn't really tell if they were sympathizing with me, but I'm inclined to believe that was not the case.

Every night Red would drink at least a six-pack of beer. Some nights he'd drink a lot more. Early in the evening he'd lament the lack of female company and say something about his wife like,

"Ah she's the greatest, the fucking greatest I tell ya and if anybody was to touch her I'd rip their fucking head off!"

However, later in the night, by the light of a mound of coals and melting beer cans, I'd watch his silhouette stumble towards his swag and hear him mumbling under his breath,

"Fucken whores, the lot of em, gotta get me a piece of skirt…"

Red loved road kill. Aside from Ned Kelly, beer, drill rigs and, "An easy piece of skirt," it was his next favourite thing. He was always hanging out for a chance to get behind the wheel of the Ute. He was always telling me he knew only two speeds: "Fast," and "Flat out," and I guess that helped him increase his kill.

"Whoooo hoooo, road kill!" he'd scream, whenever he saw a bundle of fresh skin, blood, beef and bones by the edge of the road. He was always on the lookout for animals which could be converted to road kill: kangaroos and emus, foxes and rabbits. Red wasn't too fussy when it came to road kill.

Between the camp and the rig there was one straight bit in the stretch of track which Red used to love. His eyes would light up in anticipation of it every morning. It was a good spot for making road kill because, given the opportunity, a driver could get up some speed.

On one side of the track was a wire boundary fence, on the other a thick grove of tea tree, amongst which we'd often see a family of idling emus, long-necked heads sticking out of the scrub like feathered periscopes.

"Wooooo hoooo!" Red would scream. "Go get em, Boof!"

However, Boofhead was rarely interested in heeding Red's call and fortunately for the emus even though Red would scream for it, bouncing, waving, drooling and barking like a kelpie dog, our passage to the rig was usually road kill free. However, there was one occasion when Boofhead, needing to discuss the week's drilling logs with the geologist, spent the night at another camp nearby and I found myself alone at the end of the day, with Big Red nestled behind the wheel.

He drove with a mad glimmer in his eyes, a glimmer which alluded to an opening, a long overdue opportunity, which had finally come his way and although I knew the odds were against me I tried hard to divert his attention from its obvious preoccupation. I began talking to Red about beer, drill rigs, skirt, even Ned Kelly,

"So Red, did you ever see that movie they did with Mick Jagger in the lead?"

Anything…

Anything to provoke his interest, anything to divert, to redirect his intentions, although it was to no avail, for as soon as he saw furry heads sticking out from the thick scrub, he became like a bull at a gate, and his foot, like a hoof, stamped down harder upon the accelerator. Red, transfixed, edged the Ute into a bank of tea tree, sending branches flying and a family of emus scrambling out of the scrub and into the clearing. All

I could do was click in my belt and brace myself.

With their necks twisting the less-than-intelligent birds ran as fast as they could, parallel to the stone spitting ute, and as they did I noticed Red, having perhaps an equivalent intelligence, was doing the same. Calling to them, a mad call, coaxing them, his lips mumbling, his eyes flickering frantically:

"Come on emus ya dumb fucks, come on, come on, have a go ya mugs…"

"Red," I said, "watch out for the trees Red."

"Fuck up, you!" he replied, throwing me a steely look. "I know what I'm fucking doing."

I held on, hoping Red would not get his way, wishing the emus might show some uncharacteristic sense, break, turn, escape, quickly dash behind the speeding ute to the freedom of the open bush. But it was not to be. Instead two of the emus tried to pass in front and resounding thumps to the bull bar, bone-crushing crunches beneath the wheels and an emerging cloud of grey and black feathers showed Red had got his morbid way and drew his own conclusion to his sick little game.

"Woooo hoooo, road kill!!!"

And for the rest of the night that was all I heard.

"Did ya see how dumb those bloody emus was? Like fucken dodos huh, hey, what-I-tell-ya, like fucken dodos."

I couldn't even look at him that night. I went to bed soon after the sun fell, but he didn't seem to notice. The last thing I remember, before sleep took hold, was the silhouette of the babbling madman thrown by the fire, big, and animated and decisively malicious.

"Like fucken dodos, hah, hah, haw…"

Though a large part of me felt like I should be, I was too exhausted to be worried.

As the end of the swing drew near so did the completion of the drilling program. The days remained long and hot, the nights mundane but star-filled. The pile of cans in the fire continued to grow, as did Red's angst and his brooding preoccupations.

Eventually word came from base saying we were to break camp and move the operation to a mine site five hundred kilometres to the north. Boofhead and I were understandably excited. A mining camp meant people. It meant a bar full of new people, people eager to talk drilling stories, other stories… It meant caterers and clean sheets and, though not usually in any great number, it meant women, the eye softening form of the opposite sex.

Red seemed to take the news more calmly than both Boofhead and I, though curious he remained unusually distant. There seemed to be a growing fire in his eyes, the glare of which I chose to avoid.

The next morning we were loaded and ready to leave. Boofhead assigned Big Red to one of the trucks, and as he climbed up into the cab we both heard him mutter,

"I'm gunna cause some fucking trouble tonight."

We kept in convoy. The drive was slow and relatively uneventful. The deserted highway passed and the kilometres ticked by. I followed Red. Occasionally he would pull his truck across into the empty oncoming lane. For kicks, I guessed, though wrongly, as one time an erupting cloud of eagle feathers showed there was some method to his game. "Whaaaaa hooooooo…" I could almost hear him screaming it.

On arrival at the mine-site we were each assigned our own air-conditioned room and after settling in Boofhead and Big Red made a bee-line straight for the wet mess, while I decided to go for a walk and stretch my legs.

I met Claire as she was returning from her run into the surrounding desert. She had beads of sweat across her brow and an affable smile upon her lips. She seemed petite, but it was something of a front, for I soon learnt that beneath the baggy clothes she wore was a well-trained athlete's body. As she wiped the sweat from her brow she explained how she was in training for a national kickboxing meet scheduled for a months' time.

"I'm a black belt, gotta keep fit ya know."

It turned out that she was the same age as me and working on the mine as a field assistant for a geologist team. It is fair to say I was attracted to her, her face, her figure, her smile. Everything about her was enhanced by the last six weeks I'd spent isolated from the world, from the female form, locked up with Big Red and Boofhead and their perversions. I asked Claire if I could join her for dinner and with an encouraging promptness she answered yes.

We sat together in the communal mess hall eating buttered dory fillets, potato ratatouille and sautéed leeks. But for a smattering of females the place was full of men and I couldn't help but feel a little special with Claire's attentions focused solely on me. However, as we ate, I became aware of another set of drunken eyes stealing in obstinately from amongst the mass, somebody watching us from across the room and as I returned to the salad bar for a second helping of coleslaw I found Red standing by my side.

"Nice piece weasel, are ya gunna fuck her or what?"

With my patience for his presence finally, thankfully, worn out, I replied quite simply,

"Fuck off, Red."

But as I wandered back to Claire I heard him laugh and his seedy voice whisper,

"Yeh, well maybe I'll have to do it for ya then…"

They were telling words, words I'd been subjected to for the previous six weeks, words I'd learnt to laugh off. I haven't seen Red since he uttered those words; chances are I'm not likely to run into him again. I turned my back on the industry a few months after that night and Red, by his own actions, decided to turn his back on conventional life for a while.

That night, exhausted by the long drive, I retired early. Claire went to join her work colleagues for a beer in the bar. She asked me to join her, but not wanting to seem too keen I decided to play it cool, and declined. We made a date for a rendezvous the following evening; she was going to teach me a few easy choke holds.

It is known Red was also in the bar and although he had nothing to do with Claire I can just imagine his sleazy eyes, above the mass of copper wire, honing in on her, undressing her, with each gulp of the large amount of beer he apparently drank.

Big Red was at his nastiest that night; his preoccupations had begun to boil over and the path the pressure flowed, when he eventually burst, was the talk of the camp the following day.

Later that night, as Claire lay sleeping, Red walked into her room. Her door was not locked; the safety of the camp had never deemed it necessary. She awoke, sat up in bed, and as her eyes adjusted to the shadow of the intruder in front she said,

"I think you've got the wrong room buddy."

But Big Red didn't reply, he just stood there breathing heavily then slowly closed the door. She said it again, thinking he hadn't heard, that he was just too drunk, but instead of leaving, he pounced.

He slapped her around the head, threw her back on the bed and drew a pillow over her head in a vain attempt to muffle her screams. Then as he held her throat with one hand, he reached down and ripped her pants from around her waist with the other.

"You know ya want it! You know ya want it..." was all the sick bastard said.

However, unbeknown to Red, and to Claire's advantage was her quick thinking and her hidden prowess at self-defence. And although he didn't know it, he was quick to learn, for as Red took his arms from her head in order to unbutton his pants, Claire let fly with a kick which was ferocious in strength and right to its mark and Red fell, howling, his hands to his crotch, as Claire ran past him, into more secure arms, those of her neighbour awoken by the commotion.

By the time I was wiping the sleep from my eyes the demise of Big Red was complete. Claire was on a charter flight back to the city and Red was locked in the back of a paddy wagon speeding across the desert towards a judgement day and the nearest steel barred cell.

I cursed him the whole next day for doing what he'd done, hurting a girl like Claire and destroying my own chance of a reprieve from the terrible lonesomeness I was carrying. But I knew his demise had been some time coming, I felt Red was like a storm, one which had been brewing for years. Though if a storm, (a cyclone, a hurricane perhaps?) well then I got to witness the eye of that storm, and I was glad to see its potential for destruction averted by a well-placed kick from his sick mind's desire.

FLYING
FISH

Having just crossed the equator, off the west coast of Colombia, Alec the Ox stood alone, smoking a cigarette, at the helm of his thirty three foot Hans Christian's sloop. The yacht, reimbursement from a warlord from Angola, who had acquired it from pirates in Mauritania, had been handling the windy conditions well. However the south-westerly trade, which had given him good speed for three days, had slowly backed off and after tending to his sails for most of the day, Alec decided to let them drop and acknowledge that he'd reached the doldrums. The surrounding ocean was smooth, like oil, its mirror-like surface reflected the sinking sun. His only companion, a large tabby cat with a mackerel lined coat, lazed on top of a fore hatch languidly swishing its tail.

"Cat, in the morning I'll start the engine and we'll motor away, but tonight we shall drift and celebrate life, and what finer life to celebrate than mine."

Beneath the surface, five hundred metres away, fish were swimming.

A school of dorado were cutting through the water at speed, their blunt bull noses twitching, their mouths agape, filtering the water as it raced past colourful trunks. Their stealth was fixated on their prey, flying fish, swimming just a little faster, out in front. As the dorado's pace increased they looked like long flags flapping in a blustery sea breeze, while the flying fish, bunched tighter, a ball of silver shooting through the blue sea. The only disturbance to their course was the hull of Alec's yacht, the position of which caused the flying fish to splinter and the dorado to attack and as fish erupted from the inky ocean with their wings extended wide, the falling sun was reflected, bright and sharp, off their scaly flanks, like fireworks exploding into a night sky.

Alec saw the dorado, for just a moment, and he marvelled at the vibrancy of their multi-hued flanks. The plight of the flying fish, however, the spectacle of their intuitive jump, went unnoticed. Alec was a predator, he cared little for prey and it was only a deep, dull, thud, coming from the centre of the yacht that alerted him to the arrival of one flying fish whose flight from the dorado had gone astray, and ended when it flew headlong into the yacht's mainstay.

The fish fell to the deck and gave a hearty flap, invoking the inquisition of the cat who quickly hot-footed it over, and gave it a tap. When the fish flapped again the cat pounced, a full scale attack, teeth to the head, until the fish shuddered, went limp and was dead. Then the cat dragged the slimy body back to a hollow, where it could feast, in peace, beneath the cover of the mainsail.

Alec was a big man, he had wide shoulders that dissolved into a thick, cannonball sized head. The lack of a neck, and nostrils well rounded and flared, was reason enough for the nickname, while he was also known for his temper; when angered he had a reputation for trampling everything that stood in his way. He was fifty-nine, with short grey hair and a well-trimmed moustache, which he once liked to believe, and make those subservient to him agree, made him look like Errol Flynn. One time, long ago, when wealth first came his way, he'd entertained the idea of becoming an actor, but the closest he ever got to the screen or stage was sleeping with a casting agent at a swingers party in LA, who said she'd put out the word. Alec never heard from her again, and no other offers were forthcoming.

The cat, fat and scruffy with a scarred nose and broken fang, had come with the boat. Usually Alec cared little for cats, or small animals of any description, but he'd grown fond of this one because it obviously knew how to fend for itself.

"Sharp," Alec would say whenever he returned to Tumaco port where the yacht was berthed,

"You're as sharp as a Ghurkha's blade. Your old coat doesn't fool me, the edge is in your eyes."

And it was true, even though nobody took care of it, the cat looked fatter each time.

As the last of the sun disappeared below the horizon Alec clambered about the yacht making sufficient preparations for the night, securing loose gear in the unlikely arrival of wind or swell. On returning to the helm he pressed play on the inbuilt CD player and the sounds of Philip Glass's 'Funeral of Amenhotep III' echoed out. Happy with his choice he left the splash of the feeding pelagic, gradually subsiding as darkness descended, and went below deck. He returned with a bottle of champagne, a chilled glass, a Cuban cigar and a jar of Russian caviar, the best money could buy, the golden eggs of the starlet, a gift from his friend, the Shah of Iran.

Alec shot the cork from the champagne into the ocean and poured himself a glass, caring little for another half, which bubbled over onto the wooden deck. He opened the caviar, taking to its contents eagerly, greedily, scooping out mouthfuls with his index fingers, while making short, loud, swine-like grunts of satisfaction.

When he had emptied the jar and licked clean the inside of the lid, he tossed both into the ocean, where they bobbed briefly, alongside the cork, before sinking. Alec called out to the cat,

"Come tiger, some caviar to go with your stinking fish."

He lowered his soiled hand so the cat could lick the residue from his fat fingers. With his other hand he lifted the glass, drained the champagne, filled it again, and turned his attentions to the cigar.

Alec was a successful man. He'd spent the majority of his life eating smaller fish and making a profit from peoples pain, importing and exporting being his main game. His list of vocations had included, amongst others, smuggling diamonds from Kenya to Brussels, running frozen chickens to a bird flu struck Asia, flying mining equipment from the Middle East to Nigeria and black market pharmaceuticals from Denmark to Russia. However, it was by supplying plastic landmines, bullets and Kalashnikovs to war-torn regions of the Congo, Sierra Leone and Liberia that Alec had become really big, money and notoriety. Alec's mainstay was weapons and he was one of the shrewdest arms dealers around.

Alec was born in the Ukraine, the son of a politician, a wealthy, corrupt and somewhat ugly brute from Odessa. His mother, a one-time beauty queen from Monrovia, died when Alec was five, giving birth his sister and only legitimate sibling, Vera. Alec grew up on the Black Sea where from a young age he learnt four things: how to make money, how to fight, how to fire a gun, and how to sail. Sailing was his passion, he was good at it, although he had also excelled at the other three.

An entrepreneurial freelancer, Alec sold weapons without regard for ideology, allegiance or consequence. He was a master of 'tubing,' the name given to the diplomatic channels used and abused in order to move illicit cargo around the world; weapons, contraband, people. Alec was not totally ignorant to the horror his livelihood caused, he knew his dealings had been responsible for the deaths of thousands of soldiers, guerrillas, and a handful of nosey journalists (two of which he'd disposed of personally). He also knew the weapons he sold had inadvertently killed or maimed countless innocent civilians, however Alec believed it was not weapons that caused harm but the people who used them, the people he sold them to, and it was this belief that kept Alec's conscience clear.

Alec prided himself on his perception. As far as he was concerned it was the only tool for succeeding in life and to succeed meant to win at all costs, to win no matter what, and Alec the Ox's winnings were propping up the coffers of various financial institutes from the Isle of Man to Dubai across to the Cayman Islands.

Alec had been married three times but never divorced. There was a chieftain's daughter from Nigeria, a bureaucrat's daughter from Estonia, and a warlord's daughter from Tehran. Each of the women had borne him three children, whom, though he chose to acknowledge financially, he hardly ever saw. His latest lover had been nobody's daughter, a daughter of war, a girl from Chechnya, a prostitute he rescued from a brothel he frequented in Odessa. He helped her to achieve her dream of becoming a dancer in Barcelona, where he kept her in an apartment close to Creu Coberta. One day, returning early and unannounced from a business trip to Cairo, he found her in bed with a younger suitor and not used to being dealt a taste of his own medicine, without hesitation, he sprayed the bed with a clip of bullets. By the time the authorities arrived to the bloody mess Alec was safely aboard his private jet, en route to an arms sale in L'viv.

As a result, Alec's definition of love had become somewhat jaded.

"They're all trouble I tell you cat, only good for one thing and even that is debatable."

The sleeping cat stirred, flicked its tail, yawned, then closed its eyes again.

Feeling the booze start to settle in Alec mumbled to himself while his mind ran with the memory of many a night he'd spent in red light back streets from Moscow to Singapore. Then he laughed, as he thought about the girl only two days before, the timid little creature sent to his hotel room door. He laughed and sniggered as he remembered the bloody sheets and the way she hobbled from the room, her fist holding tight the two twenty dollar bills.

"Ah cat, we should have bought that one with us."

Alec scratched at his crotch, downed his fifth glass of champagne, and as the evening slipped away and night descended he belched a breath of cigar smoke, champagne and caviar to the sky.

He threw back another glass of champagne, then another. The effervescence increased his grin and his grin cut his moon-shaped face in two. Alec, satisfied with the crude, rude memories pulsating throughout his mammoth head, lurid, horrid and to his liking, stretched his large, fat, hairy body, back over the edge of the yacht - like a whale breaching - and basked in the memories of his life so far. When he eventually lent forward to find the bottle empty, he tossed it over his shoulder into the ocean, raised himself and went to fetch another.

The night moved in, Luciano Pavarotti replaced Glass, and Alec accompanied him, crudely. Then, when Pavarotti was done, Alec, too drunk to choose another, sang communist propaganda songs that he'd learnt at school and memorised as a soldier stationed in the Crimea. The cat, unimpressed with the racket, relocated to the forward cabin.

After draining the contents of the second bottle Alec went for a third, dispatched the glass to the ocean and drank straight from the neck. At some stage he staggered to a hammock strung up above the cabin.

"Too hot to sleep inside, cat," he slurred to the sky, and with a puddle of spilt Krug drying to a sticky mess on his ample chest, Alec the Ox passed out.

Alec was drunk. He fell asleep without a care, without fearing the onset of weather, or the possibility of a passing tanker reducing the wooden yacht to matchsticks. Alec had long ago stopped worrying about death, he felt by living with death on his shoulder he'd earned the right to live a little longer. He also cared little for fate. As far as he was concerned fate was hocus pocus bullshit that gypsies spoke of, and gypsies were to be watched closely but never to be taken seriously. He was drunk, but he was Alexander the Ox and he was invincible.

At 6am Alec awoke with a shiver. The morning was not cold, the surrounding air was tropically warm. The ocean was, like the previous day, glassy and flat. It could have been the previous evening all over again, only now the sun was in the opposite direction, rising instead of setting. But unlike the previous evening, Alec was feeling somewhat less assured of himself.

For just a moment he thought he'd awoken in a different body. A serious hangover was knocking at his head, but the shiver had started from deep within and reverberated out and, in spite of the hangover, Alec wondered if he might be falling ill.

The shiver had coincided with the end of a nightmare which had driven a sensation out from deep within, a sensation that shook the very marrow in his bones. It was a feeling he'd not felt in a very long time, but it was a feeling he knew, and he knew it was called 'fear.'

"Hah," he laughed, rubbing his fingers into his crusty sleep-filled eyes, trying to deride the sensation, trying to tease it away and, turning to the cat grooming itself beneath the mainsail, its tail swishing like a dancing cobra, he said,

"Tiger, have you seen any angels pass our way this morning? I feel as though death just paid me a courtesy call."

He continued to laugh, wishing to make a joke of it, but the feeling lingered. He wondered why it would not leave, and wondered also why his acute perception was taking so long to make some sense of it all. Alec was rattled. Awakening to the world of the living Alec's body ached as though it had been beaten into the world of the departed. The nightmare was so intense his head was a pool of sweat and his bowels rumbled.

"Damn caviar," he spat.

The nightmare had delivered to him the gore of ten wars compounded. A maelstrom of severed limbs, disembowelled torsos and flattened heads, brains shot with shrapnel, quivering like meat jelly. He'd been presented with a vision of soldiers marching awkwardly, stumbling, with huge bloody bullet holes in their backs. Lines of soldiers, infinite miles long, dragging shattered limbs, severed bits behind them. Alec had also seen the tear-sodden faces of mothers nursing these bloody pieces of their broken children and he saw them waving the pieces towards him with inquiring faces.

It was more real and worse than anything he could imagine; the scenes of murder and carnage which ran through his mind were nothing short of genocide, a rampage of butchery and rape on fields of mass slaughter, holocaust, of an unprecedented ferocity.

Alec felt as though he had awoken somewhere else. All around him the beauty of a tropical ocean was dawning, but all he could see and sense was hell and, for the first time in his life, he felt it was a hell he had played an integral part in creating. He saw it, he knew it, but he fought himself desperately not to believe it.

He could not understand why the horrid visions had not slipped away when he had awoken; he even went so far as to pinch one of his fat pasty arms until it bruised just to make sure he was not still sleeping.

When the visions refused to cease Alec tried to laugh them away, but the laughter brought no relief. The laughter only compounded the aching, gut twisting sensation he felt working its way out from deep within.

It was like his mind had been infiltrated by another, as though an impostor was playing with him. Like swarming bees singing, the visions buzzed, biting, stinging. It was maddening, and no relief was forthcoming. For five minutes he held his head and wondered if he was dying, wondered if this is how one dies? But then, as quickly as a floating bubble bursts, the visions, the spiralling nightmares, were gone…

Alec clambered out of the hammock, shook his head, slapped at his cheek and fetched his cigarettes. There was one left, which he extracted and placed in his mouth, before squashing the empty packet and throwing it into the ocean. Then he pulled down his pants, hung his arse from the edge of the boat and relieved himself. When he had finished he lit the cigarette. The smoke gave him no comfort, instead it tasted foul, astringent. The taste was familiar and when he realised it was the taste of blood he spat the half smoked butt, with some vehemence, into the ocean.

Beneath the surface, five hundred metres away and heading in the direction of the yacht, fish were swimming.

As with the previous evening, flying fish, out in front, bunched tight together while dorado jacked, weaved and pushed closer. When the dorado launched their attack, the flying fish broke rank and abruptly went skyward, like flying shards of glass. All but one fish sought the sky, all but one of the flying fish - larger than the rest - with a bullet shaped body, barrelled, thickset, robust. The solitary flying fish kept its line, straight towards Alec's yacht, closely pursued by the largest of the dorado, the jaws of which were closing in fast.

Alec moved back to the helm, shook his head, scratched his matted chest and called to the cat,

"Ready yourself, you lazy feline, we're heading back to Tumaco. The doldrums are making me sick. Death surrounds me, eats at me. I feel as though I've just awoken in hell."

The solitary flying fish swam with all its might, fleeing, darting, dodging with its fins pulled in tight, but still the dorado drew closer…

Alec stood at the helm and looked at his reflection in a small mirror, kept by the wheel for shaving, but the doughy faced creature which looked back at him was not to his liking, only a shadow of the hard man he believed he would see. Although he tried to deter it, although he tried to laugh it off, he felt the fear returning, he felt it rumbling at his bones. His reflection did not deny it, it only endorsed all he was feeling, and as he put a heavy fist through the small mirror his body shook as another shiver from deep down rattled its way out.

Beneath the surface the solitary dorado had closed the gap, one more push from its muscular tail and its race would be run, the game would be over and breakfast would be served. The flying fish pulled its wings in closer, gluing them rigidly to its taut sides, and arched its back. With all the speed it had gathered eluding the dorado the surface of the ocean came quickly.

Alec swore and stubbornly bit down hard upon his lip, drawing blood. It was a feeble attempt to dissuade the fear and dissuade also a nervous chatter which had started in his teeth. His shaking hand went to the boat's ignition key.

Like a torpedo the flying fish burst out from the ocean extending its wings as it started to gain height. Instinctively the pursuing dorado flicked its tail, as though in disgust, and quickly braked its chase.

If Alec cared at all for prey then he might have been able to circumvent his fate. It is fair to say his nervous system had taken a battering, that his instinct, his perception, was far from his side and the last thing Alec remembered seeing, all too late, and before he died, was the scaly projectile, moving like a rocket, out of the corner of his eye. And although his instincts fought to return, to give him that one last chance of reprieve, the flying fish, like a Kalashnikov bullet, like David's stone sent forth to Goliath, got there first and slammed into Alec's temple with equivalent force. Alec The Ox fell...

The frenzy of the feeding fish subsided. The yacht continued to float on the glassy ocean, aimlessly. Alec's body lay awkwardly, slumped over the helm, slowly growing stiff, with the fingers of one hand still clasping the wheel. For quite some time the large flying fish flapped about, its mouth open gasping for water so near but so far, 'til its beat gradually subsided and its body also began to turn rigid.

From up above, a solitary Arctic tern broke its long flight south and descended to rest on the crossbeam of the mast. The bird looked down on the body of Alec the Ox; a predator who had never stopped the chase long enough to consider the proposition that prey, under the right circumstances, could be so detrimental to his very being. When the bird's beak opened it seemed to smile.

At noon, the cat raised himself and wandered from the bow to the helm, jumping over Alec's body, in order to get to the fish.

After two days of drifting a wind sprung up and the yacht began to rock, ever so gently, until its hull turned and its bow was pointing south. Prevailing currents had pulled it out of the doldrums and back into the realms of wind. The weather would carry the floating package, silent but for the occasional meow of the cat growing hungry, south, joined, for a while at least, by dorado in pursuit of flying fish.

ELEPHANT
CHAIR

I am sick. I cannot remember ever being so sick in all of my life. I feel as though rats have crawled up inside of me and are slowly dying. My head aches, my guts churn, my mouth is a pipe through which I puke the decomposing rats.

I have spent the last eight hours straight in a bathroom watching swallows. There's a clay nest by the light fitting above my head. They fly in, they fly out. The concrete floor beneath me is cool. The toilet is at arm's reach; I have nothing left inside me to give but still I go. My body feels like a chocolate Easter egg, like I am hollow inside and any moment I feel I may shatter and melt away.

What the hell I was thinking when I ate that steak I'll never know. Perhaps I was not thinking at all. I'd been trekking for two weeks through the Himalayas, I'd crossed a mountain pass six kilometres high. I was hungry, hell, I'd been subsisting on sand tainted dhal and rice every day for breakfast, lunch, dinner as well.

A rare steak too. Fool, times one. Served in a dirt floor restaurant by a waiter who wore no shoes. Fool, fool, times two. Waiter with a big bastard smile, with whom I had sent it back twice, but then eaten it anyway, when it was still bleeding, the colour of a monk's robe. Fool, fool, fool, times three.

There's a knock at the door.

"Jake, are you ok, can I help you with anything? You've been in there the whole day."

It is English Elsie. We met the previous evening in the lobby of the hotel, just before I went to eat my steak.

"What's that?" she'd asked the owner of the hotel, pointing to a large elaborately embroidered hardwood chair.

"Oh, Miss, it is an elephant chair."

"An elephant chair?"

"Yes, Miss, that is correct."

"What, do elephants sit on it?"

"Oh no Miss, people."

"People?"

"Yes Miss, atop the elephant's back."

"Oh really, how peculiar..."

Elsie has a heavy head of blond dreadlocks and a pierced nose. She wears a red sari and black combat boots. She tells me she has worn the sari every day since she bought it three weeks ago in Nellore. She covers the increasingly bad smell with a clay-based powder made with patchouli.

She is small, slight framed. I get the feeling, but for the heavy head of hair and the boots, she might just blow away. When trekking she lights incense sticks and secures them to the straps on her rucksack and listens to her Walkman, loaded with her only CD; the Monsoon Wedding' soundtrack.

Elsie is very good at reminding me of my predicament.

"Jake," she says, "you shouldn't be eating meat, it is dead food, cows are sacred here Jake, especially not here Jake, that's why you're sick you know, it's a karma thing."

"Thanks Elsie," I reply, "aren't those boots leather?"

I am a stubborn man. I don't want to be sick. I just want to move on. I am determined to get over it quickly, when all is said and done. I stumble out of the bathroom and Elsie follows.

"Jake you really don't look so good you know, you look a little like death, that man with the sickle, the salmon mousse."

She points a crooked finger towards my face.

I return to my room, dress and stumble out of the hotel and down the street. Elsie follows five steps behind me.

"Oh Jake, I'm not so sure if you should."

"Look, Elsie, I just need to get some water and some fresh air. I'll be fine."

"Hmmmmmm."

She continues to follow. Three hundred metres down the road, my head starts to spin. I turn around and around, performing an uncouth pirouette in the dirty street.

"Wait Jake, I'll get some water for you, wait just a second."

I watch her disappear into a ramshackle store, then I fall. When she returns she finds me in a muddy ditch by the side of the road puking bile all over a mountainous pile of buffalo shit.

"Oh Jake," says Elsie "I told you not to leave, now you're all sick again."

"Oh Elsie," I say, "I'm fine really, I just dropped something." I neglect to mention that I've soiled my pants as well.

Elsie and I leave Dharamsala four days later. It's a sunny afternoon. The road out of the mountainous town zig-zags down into valleys of thick foliage and swift rivers. The old bus, battered and beaten, displays all the scars of a hard life yet its engine labours on convincingly. The driver shows little regard for the hairpin turns and I, feeling a shadow of my former self, am equally as disinterested, caught by the haphazard rhythm that accompanies third world travel, lulled into an unsubstantiated sense of security.

I am, however, feeling slightly better. I have no appetite and my head still spins, but my guts have decided to give me a break. While the white flag I waved at my bowels (in the form of a Lomotil pack) seems to be working as well.

Elsie has decided to join me, she is on her way to Nepal. She wants to visit a national park that has elephants. I figure she is still trying to get her head around the chair. She will accompany me to the holy city of Varanasi.

We relinquish the bounce of the rickety bus for a crowded train station. There are people everywhere. Jostling for tickets we join the push and shove and are eventually rolled to the front where we are issued with third class tickets for the twenty-seven hour journey. We are allocated the last available bench seat in an over-crowded carriage. The seat will double as our bed.

The station is alive with people awaiting connections and vendors brewing tea, flipping toasted naan bread, hawking spicy lentil cakes. The train station's proximity to a local air base is felt through the reverberating rumble of departing jet fighters, blue arcs of afterburners torch the night sky.

We find a space on the siding and sit atop our packs. Elsie's mound of matted golden hair draws the attentions of young soldiers milling around a stack of khaki kit bags. She produces a sarong from her bag and wraps it close around her head, yet her blue eyes steal out and continue to allure.

"Oh Jake, can you please tell them to stop staring at me in that way."

"But Elsie," I say, "with your sari and patchouli perfume, perhaps they see you as a prospective bride."

I leave the platform to buy bottles of water from a vendor on the outskirts of the station. A lamp hangs illuminating his cart, the smell of cinnamon and coriander, the smells from recently fried morsels, hidden beneath grubby muslin, mix with smoke from idling patrons' cigarettes and slowly dance out into the humid night sky. Elsie remains under the inquisitive eyes of the male dominated crowd, until the locomotive-led mile of diesel stained carriages arrives to carry us further south.

As the train pulls away there is a full moon rising, solid and bright, in the northern sky, silhouetting all that is stationary or mobile in Uttar Pradesh. The moon is to remain our companion throughout the journey. It diminishes as the morning's light arrives, and returns with a fiery intensity with the onset of the evening.

The bench seat as a bed is less than adequate, but we are in no position to complain. The carriage is full. The floor is littered with bodies, people lean three deep on each other in the doorway, limbs dangle down outside from the roof. Still, interlopers at various stops along the way vie for a portion of our meagre seat.

The odour from the carriage toilet, an open hole to the track below, intensifies as the trip wears on, its entrance blocked by a mass of crouching bodies. I step on hands, feet, a head even, as I negotiate the crowd to the putrid hold, to squat atop the stinking hole, and watch the wooden girders on the track below flash by like falling dominos.

The banter of foreign tongues, sweat from confined skin, the colour from a multitude of saris and turbans is all-consuming. Elsie falls into an exhaustion-fuelled slumber, while I have become entrapped in sensory induced insomnia, my eyes fixated on the moon as it rides through the night.

Stops along the way are frequent but the duration is never known. Tea sellers rush through the carriage, one hand swinging a huge aluminium pot the other holding a stack of earthenware cups. The tea is milky, sweet, and tainted with cardamom. On finishing each brew the cup is discarded by throwing it from the train to smash on the track below. It is seemingly impossible to escape people in India; the first cup I throw unceremoniously explodes on the head of a Sadu meandering alongside.

Elsie eats dhal-bhat held in a banana leaf bowl and samosas smothered in chilli jam. I avoid watching her eat. My stomach twists and turns at the sight. She smiles and holds a samosa up to my face,

"Jake you have to start eating one of these days."

The jam falls and melds with the sequins on her sari. I feel myself beginning to gag, I hold my mouth and push her hand away.

The journey wears on. The heat is inescapable. The dry season is reaching its climax, soon the monsoon will be inundating the land. My head aches. I dream dreams of rain as the bodies that surround me meld to another communal afternoon doze.

As the light of the evening fades Elsie awakes again, sleep has left her rested though parched. As the train pulls out of a siding she buys an icy-pole from a young vendor who gestures to the open window. The ice melts to sticky orange streams which run down his arms. She won't get sick from this but, in a macabre way, I'm secretly wishing she will.

Eventually the train rolls into Varanasi early on the third morning of the journey. The station is chaotically packed with pilgrims, milling around idle carriages or searching for sleeping space on the platforms. We decide against heading into the city centre until the light arrives. Instead we look amongst the masses for room to sit down and rest.

The concrete is dirty, hard, but comfortably cool. The banter of small beggar children, contesting for my spare change, rings out alongside the snores of sleeping bodies. All are oblivious to the monotonous clatter of passing iron wheels. Elsie dozes. I sit upright, straight-backed, wide awake. Still I can't or won't sleep. I am filthy, exhausted, but my body will not give.

At 5am we hire a motorised rickshaw. The driver speeds through the dimly lit heart of the city and deposits us by a narrow alley leading down to the banks of the Ganges. Walking the last hundred metres our packs feel full of lead. However, as we emerge to face the holy river we are immediately awestruck by the scene which lies before us.

The holy city in all its glory is awakening. The morning sun skips across mudflats to the east turning the glass-like river to a mirror, reflecting the Ghats and lines of smouldering funeral pyres. The sounds of a sitar travel along the shore as people materialise from the antique maze of mortar and brick and meander down to the water's edge for morning ablutions. For a mile we walk as though in a dream, the exhausting weight of the train ride lifted by the ancient mysticism lapping at our heels.

I feel alive again, yet I am immediately aware of my insignificance in the scale of this town bound by enlightenment. We are spectators and although nobody sets out to demean us we are, in all our foreignness, but a second thought amongst so many seekers of divinity.

What are my concerns? What is my sickness to a world which loves and loses, a world which lives and dies on an hourly basis? What are my concerns as boats crisscross a swollen river? As sailors throw pails of ash, human gristle and human bone up into a northerly wind, which catches the remains and dashes them down, like shrapnel, into a holy river?

Sleep comes to me eventually. We find clean lodgings a short distance from the river. In the corner of the room we share is a chair. It is a large chair, a beautiful hardwood chair, with reinforced straights for securing the ropes of a harness. It is an elephant chair. I drop my pack and nestle on top of its cushioned base, warm, soft, secure.

"Oh Jake, you are far too skinny to be an elephant," Elise says. She prances around the room like a Ghoomar dancer, her Walkman aloft in one hand.

Sacred monkeys, guardians of a nearby Hindu temple, rattle at the window, though they do little to revoke the slumber which is long overdue, and the moon is nowhere to be seen.

MOROCCAN
COFFEE

The Arabs of Larache had little time for the rigours of dentistry. Their grins were brown or toothless, a legacy of hours spent deliberating over sweet and potent brews at the ancient town's many cafes.

I travelled to Morocco by boat, disembarking at Tangiers, though my stay in the port city was short. I was driven to leave by the consistent haggle of the local tourist sharks, their tactics intimidating and relentless. I boarded the first bus heading south after a finger probe at my map gave me a destination.

Larache was a maze of rustic charm, a bohemian fantasy, held in place by the crumbling limestone walls of a fortified medina. I found sanctuary in the many cafes which lined the town's central square. The customers were predominantly male, indicative of a tradition-locked society. Steely eyes and exaggerated hand gestures played through floating clouds of cigarette smoke.

They used the cafes as places to conduct business, debate current affairs, gamble at cards or just idle away the day.

To the hiss of archaic coffee machines with chrome fronts polished to a mirror-like shine moved the youth of Larache; adolescent waiters delivering tempered glasses of freshly brewed coffee or steaming mint tea, shoeshine boys loitered by the entrance, tapping their brushes on their boxes as a way of coaxing business, cigarette sellers with packets open darted among the tables and chairs, selling single butts to those in need.

To the west of the town rolled the Atlantic Ocean, to the north an inlet, a safe harbour for a small fishing fleet. The fishermen, distinguishable by their tight-fitting woollen caps, sat mending their hemp fibre fishing nets waiting for the tide to turn.

One afternoon, while walking on the outskirts of the Medina, I met a dishevelled old man collecting plastic bags to sell as scrap. In broken English he directed me to a cemetery lying untended amid scrub on a small peninsula which fell to the ocean below.

He gestured to a small tombstone lying closest to the edge of the cliff, atop a stony outcrop commanding a perfect view of the surrounding blue. The inscription read: "Jean Genet 1910-1984." The French existentialist writer died in his native France but chose to be buried in Larache. The man smiled, I stood beside him, transfixed and a little bewildered. I was half-way through Genet's novel, 'Miracle de la Rose', the book was buried in the small pack on my back.

I woke early on my final day, the crack of thunder signalling an approaching storm. It encroached on the medina, dulling the whitewashed houses and dispatching my dreams.

My last cup of coffee was strong and sweet as I waited for the bus to take me farther south, the falling rain delaying the onset of the day. As a lightning strike sent a brief moment of illumination, I wondered what other secrets waited to be uncovered beyond the historic town's facade. I finished the coffee and, using my tongue, inspected my teeth for any signs of decay.

BALI

-

THE

EXTINGUISHING

OF

FEAR

The first time I ever saw a dead body was in Bali. I was twelve years old, on my first overseas holiday with my family. One afternoon an elongated funeral tower passed by the front of the four star hotel and the colour, the crash of cymbals, the beat of drums, lured me away. Although I knew at the time I shouldn't, that I would cause my parents worry and would be reprimanded accordingly afterwards, I joined the procession, following the mayhem until it reached a clearing where the cremation was to take place. I was driven by something which lies between fear and curiosity. I was swept along for the ride by the vibrancy of the ritual display: the clouds of incense, the manic gesticulations of the pall bearers, instigated in order to confuse the spirit of the deceased and aid in his ascension.

The deceased was of a higher caste, a Brahman. His funeral sarcophagus was the shape of a bull. When the tower was lowered and opened to remove his body, I stole in to take a look. He was old. His skin was pallid, the colour of milk. His arms were folded, his finger nails long, twisted, indicative of Indonesian practice. A whispery goatee beard adorned his chin and on his head was a topi of an ornate stitch. It was just a glance, though it was all my innocence could take. I ran the whole way back to the hotel with tears falling from my cheeks.

My tenth trip to Bali was just before Christmas, post October 2002. Arriving from winter Europe I was relaxed and eager for a planned week long stopover, not unlike the times I'd had before: sun, surf, vibrant smells, culinary titbits from street side stalls.

After alighting from the plane I jostled past an extended line of people heading for the transit lounge, joining a much smaller line at a desk marked 'Immigration'.

"Christ," said a Kiwi surfer standing behind me. "I usually wait for ages to get my passport stamped here, the place must be empty." I found myself quickly hustled through, though the words he spoke remained on my mind.

Of course the thought had occurred to me; with terror alerts still high, what would it be like only a few months post Bali bombing? Would anyone be here? Would there be an increase in street crime? Petty theft? Ruthlessness? For surely the man on the street, the trinket seller, the t-shirt vendor, must be doing it tough.

As I left the airport I was greeted by smiles, though they were not the smiles I was used to. They were mournful, solemn, melancholic smiles. The friendly grace was still there, the same as always, though it was wrapped up in a cloak of confusion. I quickly reminded myself taxi drivers, vendors, the men and women in the street, those whose very livelihoods depend on the tourist, perhaps do not have the edification, or access to all the information, to understand why this is happening to them.

The place where the Sari Club once stood was two acres of cleared rut in an otherwise chaotically built up street scene. Wreaths of flowers and messages printed onto lengths of silk hung from a galvanized sheet wall, which surrounded forty square metres of hallowed bloodstained rubble. It was an eerie place. "Love Conquers Fear," read the placard, "Fuck

Terrorists" read the t-shirt, "Terrorists Don't Surf," read the sticker.

The monsoon season was beginning, the air was wet, heavy. A consistent, all-encompassing heat prevailed which did little to divide night and day. There was only the intermittent - that El Nino year rare - morning and evening downfall for relief. Swimming in the ocean was like swimming in a bath, wooden outriggers dotted the sea like cigar-shaped beads on a shimmering azure tapestry.

It was also the time when flora is in full bloom and fruits were bountiful. Frangipani flowers lay everywhere, perfumed parcels of life in various shades of yellow and red. Water lilies in limestone pots with the most subtle yet most alluring of scents. Mangoes were ripening, star fruits dangling, papaya, mangosteen, super-crunchy Chinese apples. Incense sticks burning, smouldering coconut husks, rectangular parcels of coloured sticky rice in banana leaf boats, a drizzle of rose water, offerings to the gods. Bali remained the most lush, mystical place that I have ever been to.

I returned to my five dollar a night losmen, found my surfboards, left eight months previously, still there, hired a motorbike and went surfing. On the first day I forgot that my skin was Scandinavian pale and after three hours in the water gave myself the worst sunburn I have ever had. A week later, when I began to peel, I lost my skin with a leper-like constancy.

The nights were quiet in the heart of Kuta, it was only the backpackers and surfers who frequented the restaurants. Though they afforded the sultry streets something of its cosmopolitan former self, their tight budgets would take some time to return the holiday island to its former prosperous glory. The food however, as always, was fantastic; nasi campur, nasi padang, whole fried fish in garlic, chilli and ginger, gado-gado washed down with fresh papaya or pineapple juice.

One evening, while skirting between smoky kerosene lamps of the pasar malam (night market) I met Stan, a forty-five year old surfer with the demeanour of a salty seadog. He had a jagged pink scar on his left forearm, the mark of shrapnel which struck him on that fateful October night.

"It was bloody unbelievable at the time," he said shaking his head.

"From the heat of the flash to the noise, the blast from hell, that's left me deaf in one ear. Hollywood? I tell ya, they couldn't ever create such bloody carnage…"

Then later,

"It was surfers who discovered this place, who brought it to the masses and it will be surfers who bring the people back again, 'cause the only terror a surfer cares about is the one you face when you're staring down the line of a ten foot Uluwatu freight train!"

There was a legacy of the other fear in Stan's eyes and I noticed it, briefly, before all the Bintang he was drinking pushed it away, to the back of his mind.

"It's these guys that I'm more worried about," he said, gesturing to a crowd of coffee-coloured limbs.

Stan was right in saying the Balinese deserve to be remembered when one thinks back to October the twelfth. They, by their ethnic and religious minority, were as much a target in the monstrous crime as the western victims, and without a pinch of the support most receive in the West. They live with the destruction as a constant reminder.

I flew out of Bali under the deep red glow thrown by a sinking sun. As it burned itself out on the horizon I realised, watching its extinguished glare fade, every funeral pyre has the substance to give birth to life, and the real beauty of Bali is optimism. Even though the scars left by terror shall always remain, happiness, the contours in a Balinese smile, will always prevail.

GREGORY REWEGA

TEVY

-

WHAT

A

DOLLAR

BUYS

Tevy holds back her hair to insert a dollar sign hair clip, made of cheap plastic. She wears fake pearl earrings and a threadbare cotton dress, which she pulls down as she bends to collect used condoms from beneath the bed with the pinch of two nails, showing receding polish, the remnants of red. Tevy is seventeen.

"I like it here," she says, unconvincingly.

"We all get along, no arguing, no fighting."

Tevy ventures a shallow smile and gestures out of the tiny room with walls built out of packing crate wood, towards five other young women lazing in a larger room, sitting cross-legged, combing wet hair, sipping coffee from chipped cups. They don't look up. Their attentions are distracted by the tinny sounds and blurred pictures emerging from an old TV set, which seems to have a mind of its own and is continuously jumping between channels. One of the girls gets up and frantically hammers away at buttons until the karaoke show they were watching is restored. There's a collective sigh of relief and some of the girls start to sing along.

A fan with rusty blades spins overhead, chasing away the May heat, the relentless humidity, the dust from the street, which drifts in past cheese-cloth curtains.

All of the girls are young, their enthusiasm seems strained. The joviality they show for a badly dubbed television show seems somewhat shallow, a mask for other preoccupations. At eight-thirty am the working day for most in Phnom Penh is well under way, though for the girls it is just about to begin.

Tevy returns to collecting discarded latex, crumpled on the floor, and rearranging condom awareness posters which sag from the walls, while speaking to me in broken English, a language she first heard at the beginning of her ordeal, with her first client.

"He was American, fat, with blond hair and big nose, but he pay big money!" she says with a smile.

The 'big money' Tevy speaks of equated to approximately $300 - very little of which she ever saw - split between a brothel owner, a broker and her family's well connected neighbour, who was first to notice the opportunity that lay, at play, on the other side of the fence. It cost just $300 to deflower her fifteen year old body and keep her for a week.

However, since Tevy lost her virginity and innocence to the desires of a traveling westerner, the price her body commands, two years later, has drastically reduced. She now earns 5000 riels or approximately one dollar, for twenty minutes of services rendered. In Cambodia young prostitutes are highly regarded, but they quickly become considered 'depleted.'

'Tevy' means 'angel' in Khmer, though she leads a far from angelic life. Across the stale waters of Lake Boeng Kak, overlooking the bustling backpacker haven known as 'Lakeside,' approximately fifty to seventy rickety wooden shacks make up Street 73. Brothel after brothel, five to ten girls in each, provide the cheapest place in Phnom Penh for a large percentage of working class males looking for sexual relief.

As Tevy finishes her preparations by straightening a stained, frayed, maroon-coloured sheet one of the girls calls her name. Waiting in the other room is a middle-aged man with a portly frame, squeezed into a policeman's uniform. He gives her a knowing smile and says something in Khmer, quickly. Tevy feigns a laugh, smooths down the front of her dress, and motions him into the room.

The enterprise where Tevy works is owned by a policeman, as is the case with many brothels in Cambodia. Though the police are meant to be closing down the brothels they're often on the payroll. Thirty percent of Tevy's customers are police, they pay less than most clients, if anything at all.

The owner also owns a restaurant in the centre of the city. Every evening, at around seven, his wife arrives to take his cut of the day's takings from the girls and to make sure they are securely locked in for the night. Sometimes she brings a pot of leftovers from the restaurant, which is a welcome change to the girls' other option, a food cart a hundred meters up the dusty street. The old lady who owns the cart is fat, grouchy, mean. She takes great pleasure in belittling the girls, laughing at them, as she slaps watery curry over sandy rice and purposely neglects to add the tiny morsels of meat.

Despite recent, well documented, high profile paedophilia charges laid against western sex tourists, the reality is Tevy's profession is an industry serving mostly Cambodian men. There are between 30,000 and 40,000 sex workers across Cambodia, nearly half of them under sixteen.

Because of its exceptional condition of being a country slowly recovering from the destruction of war and genocide, fifty-one percent of the population are under twenty-one. Working class Cambodian men are trapped in a violent past, living the legacy of Pol-Pot's archaic attempts to turn Cambodia into an agrarian paradise. With a judicial system only recently set up to seek justice for genocidal crimes committed over thirty years ago, in the shadows of tin-pot attempts at reconciliation, in a society that relies on ruthlessly acquisitive philosophies for direction, the future looks less than bright for many Cambodians and there is a lot to hide from. The political realms of Cambodia are full of rampant corruption and the ordinary man in the street is scared. Much of his pride and resistance has been driven into submission by his country's recent history, and many seek solace in vices, be they drugs, alcohol or prostitution…

Low income, malnutrition, poor health and illiteracy has led to a vulnerability within the general populace. While poor parenting and weak law enforcement has led to the breakdown of family groups and the exploitation, abduction and trafficking of women, children and, although rarely receiving as much attention, men as well. Tevy's older brother was trafficked to Thailand when he was just fourteen. Though he was told he had a job in construction the reality is he probably began his new life working for a chao pho syndicate, begging on the street. Her family hasn't heard from him since he left.

In a country associated with images of paedophilia, people trafficking and inexpensive, unrestricted prostitution, these daughters of Cambodia, girls like Tevy and her colleagues who work on Street 73, are in a different league again, for the prices they charge make them some of the most inexpensive prostitutes in the world.

At a dollar a time, Tevy needs at least ten clients a day to make a profit. Amongst other expenses she has to buy makeup: lipstick, eyeshadow, cheap copies of glossy brands, poorly made, which many of the other girls develop allergic reactions to.

However, perhaps the saddest price she pays is the twenty-five cents a day rent, for the saggy bed and rickety room where she entertains doubles as her bedroom at the end of the working day. From every dollar made the owners received thirty cents, and for the pleasure of living in the same dusty abode where they work, sleeping on the same stained bed where they turn tricks, the girls pay the owner seven dollars a month. It is a sad life.

Most girls send a large portion of their earnings home to their families in the provinces. Some parents know how they earn it, others don't, and too many know but don't care.

Prostitution in Cambodia is fraught with risk, over thirty percent of prostitutes contract HIV. At the brothel where Tevy works aid workers arrive with a box of five hundred condoms every fortnight, however when they are all gone the notion of protection often goes out the window.

"Some customers bring their own." says Tevy.

"Though if a customer wants to have sex without a condom, then he must pay two times."

She holds up two fingers to make her point. Most of the girls are willing to consent as long as the customer pays double.

Monthly HIV and STD checks, though they exist, are seldom encouraged like they are in the west. A free clinic passes by periodically over the month but the girls shy away from letting them in because they scare the customers away.

Within ten minutes the fat policemen is finished. He leaves the room licking his lips and wiping sweat from his forehead with a fist full of handkerchief. Tevy is only halfway through bathing when her name is being called again.

Over the course of the afternoon she is busy. As I sit, trying to look inconspicuous reading atop a wobbly chair in a corner, I count nine men periodically enter, then, about fifteen minutes later, leave her room. Initially Tevy endeavours to shower between each customer, but she gives up after customer number three.

"She is always busy, because she is pretty," sneers Bopat, another of the girls, who sits awkwardly on a chair alongside me. At twenty-two Bopat is the oldest prostitute working in the house and her thin limbs and emancipated face hint at her fondness for Yaba, or 'crazy medicine,' as the strong street amphetamine is known. Bopat's pupils are the size of pinpricks, her attentions are focused on the front door. She is high, she has only had two customers and she needs a few more to feed her drug habit as well as make ends meet.

Bopat has developed a skin disorder which manifests as a collection of red, weeping ulcers running up and down the back of her legs. She doesn't seem too fazed. The sores remain hidden when she lies on her back. Until the next free clinic passes by, in about three weeks' time, she has little option but to keep on taking customers. She has a habit of repeating the things she says two or three times. Tevy tells me she thinks Bopat is slowly losing her mind.

The final time I see Tevy she is tired but happy. Her last customer, a regular, has bought her a new dress and with it on she looks pretty. However, she is no longer in a mood to chat about her livelihood; she looks as though she is somewhere else. But where does a young lady who knows little other than the life she leads go for solace? I wonder as I ready myself to leave the brothel made of packing crates and tin for my own world, one wide and full of opportunity. I am caught by the web of repetitious days Tevy faces.

As we embrace she allows one last genuine cheeky smile. I endeavour to ask her where she goes to escape her working life, but all I receive is a confused brow and cursory remarks,

"Oh, I go to the park, sometimes, with the girls, and sometimes we go to the city, the river too…"

I thank her for her time and as I leave the darkness of the rickety shack for the crazy evening traffic a heavy monsoonal thunderstorm breaks overhead. The question will not be answered. Instead I decide Tevy's utopia, the place where she escapes to, may just be a blank place, an empty place where nothing she knows, or has become accustomed too, exists.

WHAT
MAKES
A
DANISH
KEBAB

FOREIGNERS, PLEASE DON'T LEAVE US
ALONE WITH THE DANES

reads a neon poster peeling from a brick wall across the road from my apartment.

"You have got to see this, this is disgusting, really! Come and check this out."

I joined Joe, my friend the medical student, in front of the TV. He pressed play on the remote control. I couldn't understand what was going on, so Joe interpreted. There was a sixty-something bearded guy, not exactly a picture of health, carrying more than a few extra kilos. He looked to be in some discomfort, continuously moving from a reading chair in a darkened lounge-room to a small toilet in a hallway, a newspaper rolled up under one arm.

"Constipated," Joe said. "Seriously constipated."

Shot moved to the man lying in a hospital bed. Shot showed doctor's hands appraising man's swollen belly. Shot moved to said man on bed being wheeled into surgery. Shot moved to a young doctor attired in surgery garb explaining the procedure.

"Uhhh, he's so constipated they have to operate, they say everything else they have tried has proven fruitless."

The doctor on the screen continued to talk, all gobbly-gook to me. His eyes opened wide, his arms thrown out to emphasise, to make a point, of something with his hands. Shot cut to a large, brown, brick shaped object seemingly melting on a surgical tray - it looked like meatloaf.

"Solidified turd," said Joe. "Faecaloma."

He pointed to the screen laughing, his eyebrows bent in disbelief.

"The doctor says it weighed four kilos."

"Christ," I said. "I think I am going to be sick."

"Kebabs! The patient says kebabs are his favourite food..."

There were always people belching down below in the street, usually while I was trying to sleep, late at night, early in the morning. There was a kebab shop downstairs, I guess that didn't help, and a bar next door. That says it all really.

In the afternoons the smell of the grilling meat would waft all the way up to the apartment I inhabited on the fifth floor, and in the early mornings the smell was accompanied by the 'clicketty-clack' of the horse-drawn Carlsberg truck.

An infamous nightclub, Vega, was just down the road, so on the weekends the kebab shop did a roaring trade. The sticks of meat, d¬oner and chicken, turned slowly on the upright rotisserie by the window, in order to entice people passing by on the street outside. I saw these greasy parcels looking luscious, oozing juice, fat-fed gravy, at lunchtime, in the evenings, or late in the night. But I also saw the same sticks of meat early in the morning, as leftovers from the night before, when they looked less appetising: rotisserie turned off, the soft glow of the grill gone, fat congealed into thick globules of lard.

Ali the Turk owned the kebab shop; he was there all the time. He was thirty years old, thickset, with a hairless head, a big nose and wide brown eyes. During summer Ali liked to go to the beach, on the rare days he took off, and on his days on he would talk about girls. Ali liked the summer because all the girls are wearing short skirts.

"Your girl, is she good with the cooking? Is she good with the cleaning?" he asked me one day.

"Actually Ali, I do most of the cooking," I replied and watched as a look of astonishment rippled across his brow.

"Oh," he said taking it all in, before raising a finger to his puckered lips, bringing his head a little closer, breaking his mouth to a smile and saying,

"It's ok, I won't tell anybody."

He slapped me playfully, patronisingly, on the shoulder. I let it ride.

"I'm always working, always working," he said, which seemed to be true, but he also spent a lot of time laughing into his mobile phone and smoking cigarettes as well.

Joe turned the TV off and went back to his newspaper. I diverted my attentions from my book and looked over his shoulder at the picture which accompanied a story from the recent Mermaid Pride, Copenhagen's annual gay parade. The picture showed a guy standing naked, spread-eagled atop a float, wearing nothing but body paint and a pair of shin high boots. His dick swung freely, painted in coloured bands, stripes to match his painted face.

"Ha," Joe said laughing.

"What?"

"It says here some of the more fanatical members of the Muslim community were arrested for trying to stone them."

I met Hussein at the gym.

"You're not from around here, are you?" he said.

"How'd you guess?"

"Because you smiled at me," he replied. "The Danes are not in the habit of smiling at strangers."

Hussein's family, originally from Egypt, had moved to Denmark fourteen years previous. Hussein was tall and lean with a shaved head and the most amazing emerald-coloured eyes. Eyes that moved with a hypnotic allure, eyes that threw a swift net of embrace, commanding attention, a hold which was very difficult to escape.

Hussein studied computer science. On graduating he obtained a job working for an airline as a logistics officer. For five years he travelled the world, before leaving the job, craving a change. He was restless, searching for a challenge, looking for something more fulfilling.

I spent a sporadic three weeks with Hussein, before he traded the Danish sea mist for the heat of a holiday in Suez. On the night before he left we rode to an enclave called Christiania, on an island in the heart of the city. The old hippie commune is Copenhagen's little Amsterdam, where the sale of grass, hashish was somewhat overlooked by the authorities.

We drank beer, Hussein smoked a joint. We talked about life with the Danes and being a non-practising Muslim amongst others more adherent to the law. He enlightened me to the difficulties he occasionally encountered for no other reason than being a dark-hued male in a blond haired, blue eyed society, a society which was relatively slow to embrace refugees, immigrants, asylum seekers.

"Jutland cops, man, they are a thorn in my side. They pick me up all the time, give me tickets for something as lame as riding my bike on the footpath."

He smiled, a matter-of-fact smile,

"Pah. You know it's crazy, I tell them, look I've only gone twenty metres, I wasn't even riding it, I was just coasting along. Simple hey, one would think. But they don't want to know about it and they are impossible to argue with. They just tell me, 'This is the law in Denmark. This is the way it is done here, if you don't like it, well, then you should go live somewhere else.' It makes no difference to them that I have been living here for fourteen years."

I had to sympathise with Hussein, especially when I thought about the way I rode around the city; no lights, hopping from pavement to pavement, buckled wheel sliding, right hand side, left hand side, whatever side. I was certainly no model for convention, my observance of the rules was hardly austere. I'm not boasting, but I was never stopped by the police.

"So you're not a practising Muslim, huh?" I asked him.

"Na, I mean I respect the religion immensely. I'm ethically motivated, I respect the moral outlook, and I'm intrigued by its ascetics, however, I don't prostrate myself in homage to Allah four times a day and even though my family are a little more serious, like many Muslims, they don't take such a hard-line. Whenever my dad and I fly down to Egypt together and the stewardess serves the ham sandwiches we just look at each other and say, 'Nah, smoked turkey.'"

Hussein showed me a scar on his forehead, the result of a racially motivated attack the previous Christmas Eve. An unknown attacker jumped out of a bush, called him 'Black scum,' told him to go back to his own country, then cracked him across the head with a beer bottle.

He told me about the time he tried to sell his car. How he awoke one morning to find, alongside the For Sale sign, somebody had painted a large swastika and a racial slur. He drove the car down to the police station, they took his details and shrugged their shoulders.

Hussein took it all in his stride. He enlisted a matter of fact attitude while pulling a wide smile. A smile which said, I can't change the way people are and why should I bother trying anyway?

Hussein lived in an inner city suburb called Norrebro, which was chosen for religious vilification by an evangelistic preacher called Moses Hansen. The self-proclaimed 'Parson of the Lord' had been causing quite a stir due to a series of 'sanctified' walks he had been making throughout the streets of the suburb, streets which housed the city's largest community of Arab minorities.

Hansen undertook his pilgrimage of Norrebro with a wooden cross slung over his shoulder, stopping along the way to deliver a sermon or two.

He said he was preaching to rid the suburb of its Islamic spirit, to restore the purity of Danish blood, Danish virtue and to re-establish Christianity. Wherever he went there was always a huge police presence to make sure the heckling opposition which followed him did not get out of hand. On the one occasion I happened to bump into Moses on a holy walk the police presence outnumbered the whistling protesters by about two to one.

Joe told me Moses was a sixties throwback, a drug-fucked hippy, saved when he saw the light. The light took the form of a message from God telling Moses his pregnant girlfriend would give birth to a daughter and she would be born on a Tuesday. When all unfolded as predicted, Moses was saved. He relinquished the booze, drugs and rock-n-roll, changed his name, and redirected his attentions to Christ. He then undertook a vocation of sermonising against what he saw as the scourge of his beloved Aryan society, the pawns of an inaugural immigration policy, all of who happen to be dark skinned devotees to the word of Allah.

Most Danes saw him as he was, a religious nutcase, a lost soul searching for redemption. However, and unfortunately, most did not mean all.

I left Hussein after a phone call from his Norwegian girlfriend suggested he should spend his last night in Copenhagen with her.

I rode back to Vestebro, my suburb, inner city also, a once unruly postcode, which had recently become fashionable. Apartments were sought after and hard to come by. Red lights still adorned a few of the shop fronts. It was a good place to go if you were chasing a sex aid, equally so if you're looking for a quick bite of Thai, Indian or Greek.

I reached the apartment block and parked my bike. Ali was lolling out the front of the kebab shop smoking a cigarette.

"Hey man whatta-ya doing?"

"Just had a beer with a friend across at Christiania."

"Ahhhhaaa," he laughed. "You must be hungry then, huh?"

He threw it with a wink.

"No Ali, really, I'm fine, straight as a…"

"Man, don't try and kid a Turk, I know what goes on there. Come on, I make you a good kebab, a special kebab, just for you."

He waved his arm, ushering me inside. Memories of a melting brick on a surgical tray flashed inside my head.

"Come on man, get in here, special kebab, on the house, just for you!"

'Ahhh, what the hell,' I said to myself following him in. He got the first and last laugh, however; the hidden chilli made me gasp.

KANDY
FOR
THE
SOUL

Reflection

I had only felt the tantalising rewards of meditation once. I was a secondary student at an all-boys Christian Brothers school. Part of our curriculum involved regular studies of the Catholic faith and on one occasion a visit to a city monastery for a day of retreat and reflection. By way of introduction one of the teachers from the school took it upon himself to conduct a short course of meditation. I always respected this particular teacher for his un-blazoned faith, tolerant attitude and because, unlike many of the ageing Christian brothers, he appreciated a joke.

After being ushered into the dark belly of the monastery's chapel we were seated in the pews and asked to direct our attention to the centre of our body. Of course, such a suggestion to a group of forty pubescent schoolboys was like a red rag to a bull and bound to be met with ridicule, with no greater offender than me. However, for some reason, I felt drawn to participate.

He guided our concentration to our limbs, toes, fingers, heads, then our chests and eventually, more specifically, to our breathing. Afterwards we were directed to establish space. By letting idle thoughts flow by in space, we were encouraged to forego any thought at all, and, without thought, just be, breathing in a thoughtless realm of nothingness. Later I learnt there is much more development necessary in order to reap the rewards of meditation but, if for only a few moments, I seemed to get it: a spacious zone where one can just be, uninhibited by thought. Like an ocean gale blowing full and strong, it was pure, invigorating, refreshing. It was freedom, another world. All I knew or had known was irrelevant.

The experience was short lived. I quickly returned to adolescence and 'my way' of becoming in adherence to the directions of a modern world. I never really reflected on or questioned what I'd felt. I didn't have the edification. When searching for the justification I put it all down to a slip of nature, a twist of the mind.

Mangosteen

The purple pods reminded me of passionfruit from the outside, though the centre was substantially more sweet and luscious than the bitter tang of passionfruit. The vendor rolled his head when I questioned the price. The roll of the head would take some getting used to, a gesture which I perceived to mean no that actually meant yes.

"10 rupees," I said again.

"But yes sir that is the price, for now is only beginning of the season for mangosteen."

His cordiality was easy to take, a breath of fresh air, ringing out in direct contrast to the indifference at play in the north of the island.

I had arrived in the darkness of a new moon, but by morning, with my jet lag subsiding, a whole new fantastic world lay before me, painted increasingly brighter by the light of day.

There was not a lot to Midigama, just a smattering of rickety wooden shops and a couple of salt stained hotels providing accommodation to a small group of foreigners. Each morning I sat down to watch the ocean, twenty metres from the porch of my room, as I poured rich, high quality tea from a cracked and blackened china pot into a china teacup.

There was still a touch of the old Raj to Sri Lanka, surreal, taken next to the roll of the steamy Indian Ocean, the sway of coco-palms, the creaking of the dilapidated hardwood hotel, buffeted by the ever present trade winds which blew across the ocean: hot, heavy, relentless.

For four mornings I let the wind drag my recent life away as I watched fisherman negotiate a heavy swell falling viciously upon the outside reef. In the evenings I sampled their catch, baked with chilli, coriander and various other spices, but in the mornings it was always the luscious mangosteen.

I was lonely. I missed a girl who was eight thousand kilometres away and all I could think about was my decision to leave her and come to Sri Lanka alone. I had arrived with the intention of writing a story about recent Norwegian peace accords in the north of the country. My intention was to capture the common man's opinion, his thoughts, his optimism, if any, for the future. I wanted to write about peace, reconciliation, friendship, love.

But after arriving, I didn't feel like doing any of that. All I really felt like doing was sitting on the porch, drinking tea and thinking about Anna, my love, eight thousand kilometres away. With so much distance between us, and no fixed plans for a reunion anytime in the near future, I was beginning to wonder how much longer she would be mine.

The sway of coco-palms helped to distract me. I sensed the trip may be less about finding optimism from war and perhaps more about finding me.

Tirol was from Japan; a student of archaeology and a junkie - the nicest I had ever met. He was renting the only room on the second floor of the hotel. He told me he felt most at ease when he was alone. Tirol was tall and lithe, all skin and bones. He kept his hair short, neatly parted and wore glasses, which gave him a certain air of authority. I could picture him wearing a suit, riding a Tokyo train with briefcase under arm, home to a small apartment and a wife cooking a dinner of katsu.

This was his sixth time to the island. He was studying the Sinhala ruins in the North, although, he confided, with an addict sparkle in his eye,

"I also come for the brown sugar."

Tirol always had a cigarette perched between his lips. In the evenings he paced along the beach, smoking and looking out to sea, with the demeanour of a sailor's wife waiting for a ship to come in.

At other times he would sit for hours on his balcony drinking tea, a book in his hand, but again, looking out to sea. I knew he was stoned, it was obvious, though he never went out of his way to show it. He was harmless, I got the feeling he had not been at it for very long.

"Tirol, why are you always staring out to sea?"

"Because it is flat, strong and responsive to change."

"What do you mean?"

"Like a canvas is to a painter; I can make my own pictures…"

One afternoon, after much deliberation on his part, I convinced Tirol to join me on an excursion to a small island set in the wide bay of Welligama, half an hour's tuk-tuk ride from the hotel. Perched atop the island, like a castle atop a mountain, was a two storey colonial style mansion once owned by the writer Paul Bowles.

The stately abode was sold long ago to a wealthy local from the port of Galle who had converted it into an exclusive guesthouse. A sandbank leading out to the island was only passable on the lowest of tides. Tirol and I tucked our shoes out of sight beneath a bush, rolled our pants high and waded out to a whitewashed pier where we rang an old brass bell which awakened the idling gateman. I was eager to have a look around, to see something of the view Mr Bowles would have contemplated during the lethargic drag of tropical afternoons, but it was not to be. The gateman, a small middle-aged man with a gym built torso and oiled moustache, was firm in his resolve not to let us in. It was no use telling him I was Bowles' long lost nephew; he had no idea who Paul Bowles was. Instead, he just laughed, shook his head and waved us away.

We waded back, collected our shoes and hailed another tuk-tuk. Tirol was anxious for his evening fix and I needed to pack. I had decided to leave the coast the following morning for the hill country and a city called Kandy.

Train

At 5am I stood on the platform of the Welligama train station. The town slept, but the station was alive with long lines for third class tickets. I bought a second class ticket uncontested and joined the yawning throng to wait for the morning express to Colombo.

Crows screeched a clamorous welcome to the morning. A flight was perched on the twisted branches of an ancient banyan tree by the siding. The call to prayer started up from a nearby mosque and the wandering sounds of reverence echoed across the platform, providing a sweet break from the harsh calls of the crows. The crows, as though somehow aware of the significance of the call, were silenced, but as soon as the devotional wailing finished they started over.

My intention was to catch the train to Colombo with enough time spare to make a connection to Kandy. The train clattered into the siding. School children pristine in white, women draped in colourful saris and men, their heads enveloped in smoky clouds, the morning's first cigarette, pushed aboard to take up the empty seats.

The first half of the journey was uneventful, darkened shadows outside materialised as seaside villages awakening and night became day. My mind drifted in and out of consciousness lulled by the train as it rocked along the uneven track and the deep, salty smell of tropical ocean. At one stage a fleeting dream of derailment hovered in my mind before a twist in the line snapped me awake. Four hours after boarding the train pulled into

Colombo. I stretched myself back to life and shuffled out to buy an onward passage to Kandy.

With an hour to fill I wandered the neighbouring streets before settling behind a table in one of an assortment of small teahouses, all bustling with a varied collection of commuters. I drank two cups of sweetened black tea, ate a couple of fried lentil cakes and one powdery samosa. The samosa was cold, the lentil cakes warm, suffused with an awakening chilli spice.

A group of students, four boys and two girls, all well-groomed, dressed in shirts, long skirts or slacks, sat nearby. The girls' hair was either tied back or wound tight into plaits; the boys' parted and held in place with cream. They ate plates of dhal with chunks of bread, ripped from two rapidly shrinking loaves lying in the centre of the table.

A young boy stood in a corner, surrounded by a glass booth, flattening balls of dough. There was a continuous slapping noise as he manipulated each parcel, expertly throwing it down against the wooden bench, before pasting it with filling and folding it into a roti or a samosa. He had an immature moustache, diligent hands and wore a tight sports singlet with stonewash jeans. The singlet stuck to his perspiring back, and when he smiled he showed blackened teeth.

On the train to Kandy my berth was opposite a young monk. I peeled mandarins and shared the segments. He smiled, accepted gratefully, but refrained from conversing. The track had less of a roll and the ride was more comfortable.

Halfway through the journey a dishevelled looking man boarded the train and began roving up and down the carriage. He wore a grubby white shirt tucked into a pair of washed out army pants. Occasionally he stopped at a window, undid the latch, opened it, and yelled incoherently, seemingly to the surrounding jungle. After about half an hour he tired of this game and nestled onto the edge of my seat. He was small and lean with a twisted face and a mouth full of rotten betel-stained teeth. He slumped forward but did not seem particularly old, his head he held aloft, his eyes flickered at an irrational pace.

His English was poor and difficult to understand. I endeavoured to find some common ground, I fought to comprehend all he had to say, even though it was obvious I didn't. At one point he started beating at his breast and repeating,

"I proud Sinhalese, good citizen!"

He continuously stood up, sized up the carriage, then sat down again. Looking over my shoulder at a map of the country in a book I was reading, he cocked his finger, gun-like, towards the north. I realised the legacy he carried was born of war. Then he lifted a worn trouser leg and I was confronted with the skin pink fibreglass of a prosthetic leg. He hadn't limped or faltered in his mad passage up and down the train. As I was genuinely taken back, he seemed to mellow and relax. Then he smiled, adjusted his pants and the artificial limb disappeared from sight.

I no longer thought of him as intoxicated or deranged, even though he may have been both. I had misinterpreted him altogether. The scars of war lay everywhere in Sri Lanka.

Throughout my disjointed conversations with the man, the monk showed an indefinable interest, smiling gracefully, peacefully, equally at the veteran's intent and my struggle to empathise. He was somehow a part of the exchange at the same time remaining unfathomably distant.

Kandy

When the train pulled into Kandy I lost sight of the amputee and the young monk in the bustle of commuters alighting onto the station's platform. I hailed a passing taxi. The driver pushed out into seemingly impenetrable afternoon traffic, followed my directions and delivered me to a small guesthouse run by exiled Burmese monks.

An inconspicuous wooden door opened in to a small sanctuary, away from the noisy street. A postulant with a beaming smile escorted me through a rustic courtyard; maroon robes hung drying in the sun. He showed me a spare room usually reserved for visiting monks. The sparse simplicity of the room invoked the austerity of a monk's life, four walls and a mosquito net covering a hardwood bed. The passage of feet had left the rendered bathroom shiny and smooth, clean and uncomplicated. When I nodded my assent he smiled, clapped his hands and bounded away leaving me to settle in.

Jomson was the caretaker, 80 years old with a silver head of hair and a face lined by life, lines which turned to furrows every time he laughed, which he did often. His laugh was intoxicating. He wore a seventies style safari suit, smoked rough hand-rolled cigars, and drank cup after cup of heavily sugared black tea.

At first I thought Jomson a touch senile. His stories ran off on long-winded tangents which were hard to follow, yet compelling. I was not quite sure if he was telling the truth, but the truth didn't seem to matter. He commanded an overwhelming respect from all of the monks and was forever making well intentioned jokes at their expense. I was so captivated by his consistent banter I was unable to take my leave, even after my sixth cup of tea, when my bladder seemed about to burst.

One story he told concerned a jet full of Hindus who tried, unsuccessfully, to ascend to heaven by flying their chartered plane into the summit of the hallowed mountain, Adam's Peak.

"The pilot of the jet, chartered in Deli, thought himself an angel flying the people to Vishnu, iva, R ma, Krishna… and with the faith of all aboard he tried to scuttle the plane on the mountain's summit. They believed by doing so everybody would procure direct passage to a rewarding afterlife, a life steeped in gold and prosperity, but alas!"

Jomson raised a long finger to his temple,

"The plane missed its mark. The pilot, not such a good pilot, some say a drunkard, a bad pilot really, flew into another, less significant, slope nearby."

There was nothing which led me to believe such an event had actually occurred, yet the fervour with which Jomson spoke about the mountain made me rethink my immediate plans. By the time the afternoon's light had started to fade I had decided to climb Adam's Peak.

From one whimsical muse Jomson's thoughts drew him off on others. Adventurous tales suggesting a fixation with other plane crashes of the past.

"…Once, another plane, full of Christians only, fell short of the runway, ploughed into a deep pocket of ocean, and as the crumpled carriage began to sink and the passengers fought to escape, to stay afloat, a wealth of creatures rose to feast on the drowning bounty."

His eyes opened further, his arms went wide,

"Sharks fifty, sixty, seventy feet long, with rows of teeth and eyes of fire…"

I let him ramble then told him of my decision to travel to the peak the following day.

"Ah yes," he said, "you must. It is a most important, a most magical place, a shining light for all divinities, some say a porthole, a gate, to heaven. However, do not be disillusioned my young friend, remember, heaven is many things to many people. I shall tell you one more story, just one."

I leant back and crossed my legs to reduce the pain in my bladder. I was expecting another long-winded tale and he did not disappoint. However, far from crazy, it was somewhat profound and I returned to my room that evening with much respect for the philosophical old man called Jomson.

"My friend, a mixed group of humans is placed on the most beautiful of tropical islands; pristine, untouched and abundant in all forms of flora and fauna. The most lush, exotic flowers, the most colourfully feathered, sweet-voiced birds. No breath of wind blows to destroy the ambience of the fish-splashed sea or the golden sands which line its shores. The varied group is enchanted by the island. Each has eyes longing in one way or another, each sees the possibilities of the island in their own special way. The Western child, young and full of innocence, gazes out and sees a wonderful playground, his mind adrift with television born adventures, the chance to live in a realm of fantasy. The capitalist sees profit; hotels dwarfing coco-palms, marinas, cruise ships, casinos, money, money, bundles of cash. The socialist envisages a community where comrades can work side by side, brothers in arms, a dream to complement the beauty of the surroundings, a dream within a dream. Lovers' heart's explode with joy, faced with their very own Blue Lagoon. The model sees a place to nurture her winter tan. The young man a place to party, drink, meet women, play football on the sand. The writer seeks a pen, to write in an old man to go with the fish and the sea. The racist sees a dumping ground for all the bad blood affecting his narrow world. The poor see a chance to prosper, good soil, a chance to eat. The refugee sees safety, a place to call home without persecution. The dictator sees a vision of grandeur where he stands taller than all the rest. Surfers see waves. Hermits see enlightened days. The farmer smells the soil. The biologist sees months of studious toil. While some think they're in heaven, the Buddhist monk sees enlightenment. The deaf are able to hear, the blind are able to see and the otherwise impaired dream their own dreams without the constraints of physical or mental irregularity…

You see, my friend, each person has their own sense of morality, their own reasoning of right or wrong and each chooses their own path to reach their ideals. How can there be any easy answers to lengthy questions when everybody is always seeking a different truth? Man created diversity, now man must live the legacy… However, my young friend please remember, somewhere deep down in all of humanity - if I trust what my soul strives to tell me - everyone has this morality, however it is perceived or interpreted, and therein lies a universal lock to be opened by the right key…"

Footprints set in stone

The smaller train to Adam's Peak rocked back and forth up and out of Kandy into surrounding tea plantations. A throng of Tamil women, dressed in bright saris, made their way along stepped terraces, adding patches of colour to the lush green tapestry of thriving bushes. Children hung their heads from carriage windows teasing dogs meandering by the side. Men sat engrossed in, and confined behind, the wide spread of newspaper. The guard of the train was splendidly dressed in a uniform of cricket-like whites. He alighted at each station to oversee departing passengers, signalling the driver with a whistle and coloured flags held aloft in his outstretched hands.

I disembarked at a quiet settlement called Hatton, boarding a rickety bus which carried me up a long winding road to Dalhousie, a pilgrims' town, built at the foot of Adam's Peak. The vegetation of the hill country continued to allure, such a sensuous green, making everything seem perpetually ripe.

It was late November. I had chosen to climb early; the season runs from December to April. At times the whole town heaves under the weight of devotees who come to make the ascent. Stalls lined the streets. Lazy vendors propositioned me, half-heartedly, trying to sell sweets, toys, hats, fluorescent piggybanks: appeasements to the gods, encouragements of good fortune. They had a long season to come and each stall was full of goods.

Passing a small guesthouse an elderly lady pottering around a collection of small tables called me in to drink some tea and sit out the rest of the afternoon.

Beneath the guesthouse was a small windowless stone hut, a communal compound for the surrounding tea plantations. As the sun set a collection of Tamil women, their saris dirty from a day in the fields, arrived with baskets of woven bamboo laden with green tips. The baskets hung from their backs by leather straps hitched across their foreheads. There was a lot of good humoured laughing as they formed a line and a merchant, dressed neatly in a white shirt and pressed slacks, with parted hair and a well-groomed moustache, helped relieve them of their burden. He hung each basket from a set of scales suspended from the overhang of the hut, then dealt out rupees accordingly. Each woman questioned the amount paid, bemoaning the dealing hand and eyeing the other, heavy with notes.

In order to watch the day break from the top of the peak the best time to start the climb is in the early hours of the morning. Before setting out for the climb I ate from a banquet of seven different curries, prepared by the family who ran the guesthouse. Then I slept for four hours on a mattress laid out in a quiet corner of the dining room.

The conical summit of Adam's Peak terminates in an oblong platform. At the top is a large hollow, five foot four inches by two foot six inches. The resemblance to a human foot accounts for its eminence. Legend says Adam left the hollow when he ascended to heaven after standing atop the mountain, repentant, on one foot, for one thousand years. However, other religions also claim its eminence believing it to have been formed by Lord Shiva, St Thomas, the Buddha, or Mohammad and as a result a collection of shrines on the mountain play host to a variety of divinities. The peak is often referred to as 'a cathedral of the human race.'

I set out to the summit, on my own, at two the next morning following a narrow trail through a lush gully leading to an ancient stone staircase which wound up into the darkness. Tea stalls, set up intermittently on the edge of the stairway, dispelled the darkness with harsh light thrown from florescent tubes. Most of the stalls were closed. The owners of those open idled inside on wooden stools, gazing out from the light with the blank look of blind men.

I hiked at a fast pace, sweat formed on my brow. I reached the summit in under three hours. I had outdone myself, having an hour and a half to wait before the sun arrived. The chill from the morning wind sent me to shelter in a tea stall. I drank hot milky tea and ate banana cake as the owner jumped about smiling, waving his hands and speaking to me in Hindi. I returned his smile but did not understand a word he said.

Eventually, the sun arrived and bells rang out from each corner of the summit calling the faithful to prayer. A miscellany of ceremonies began and the fragrance of incense filled the air. Hindus, Buddhists, Muslims and Christians grouped together to watch the sun expose the view. Distant peaks became islands adrift on a sea of cloud. The lights of Colombo, far off on the coast, faded then expired. Prayer flags fluttered as everybody huddled, with the same intention, to soak in the warmth of the sun; a unity of diversities, perhaps enough to awaken doubt in even the most stringent atheist. As the sun climbed, ceremonies ended and everybody began leaving the peak to face the rest of the day alone. One long procession of the morally compensated filled the stairs, heading down.

I left the village soon after descending. As I waited for the bus in a ramshackle restaurant I was treated to the hospitality of the local police chief, who showed an inquisitive interest in my travels. He was tall, jovial and carried an air of authority, which he demonstrated to the young waiters with a click of his fingers. He insisted on paying for my curry lunch saying,

"Sir, as I am heading in the same direction as the bus, you must ride with me."

We drove out of the town in an old model Ford, decaled in blue and white. He showed little regard for the hairpin turns and blasted oncoming traffic with his horn. He was eager to impress me and kept speaking about his eldest daughter whom he was convinced I should meet. I just smiled and mentally willed him to slow down. He asked me to join his family for dinner. I made a lame excuse about having to meet someone.

"A girl?"

"No, an associate from work," I lied.

"Ah, good, very good. But when will you have time to meet my daughter?"

I told him I would be back in a few days. When we reached the train station he embraced me like an old friend and handed me his business card.

"When you come back, you call me, I collect you, then you come stay at my house. You can use my motor bike, my wife will feed you, and also," he winked, "you can get to know my daughter..."

By the time I got back to Kandy it was dark. The climbing of the holy mountain had taken its toll. I rode a tuk-tuk to an Indian style restaurant. The long train ride had left me with a voracious appetite, which I satisfied with a thali, washed down with a banana lassi.

I left the restaurant chewing a mouthful of aniseed and set out on foot towards the city's artificial lake, built at the monarchy's height, as a focal point to the ancient kingdom. I passed the Temple of the Tooth, a sanctuary for the national palladium: a tooth, plucked from the Buddha's body as it lay atop its funeral pyre.

I found the Buddhist publication centre positioned on the northern perimeter of the lake. A quietly spoken middle-aged man ran the office. With his thick glasses, parted hair and a tatty cardigan, he looked like a librarian. After my visit to Adam's Peak I had decided to undertake a course in meditation and Jomson had told me the centre could help me find a place where I could undertake a retreat. The curator outlined the daily routine of Nilambe, a meditation centre an hour and a half's drive into mountains south of Kandy. He explained the centre was set on a high ridge overlooking a tea plantation and said,

"There is no phone, the only way to join the course is to arrive in person."

I thanked him and left with a roughly drawn map and directions, transcribed for me into Sinhala. I walked back past the lake and followed another road which led me back to the guesthouse.

Jomson was full of questions. I was feeling exhausted and fought the pull of sleep to sit with him, to answer. Eventually a young Finnish couple arrived providing him with a greater audience, so I snuck away to the monk's room where I quickly fell asleep and dreamed dreams of footprints set in stone.

Space

Early the next afternoon I sat in a noisy tuk-tuk on my way to Nilambe. As we left the city I asked the driver to stop at a shop where I could buy an umbrella to safeguard against mountain rain. He took me to his uncle's stall.

The ride was long, the route all uphill, the small engine laboured.

My young driver didn't really know the way, so we stopped to inquire at shanty roadside shops. As he asked for directions I bought us king coconuts and we drank the sweet juice through straws. The afternoon was warm, the sun played off banana palms, the vinyl door of the tuk-tuk flapped against my leg.

Eventually I was deposited at the start of a cobbled path. We argued over the fare and the young driver accelerated away with a riled look in his eyes. As I donned my pack and started up the steep path I was joined by a couple of school children, returning home to their parents' lofty abodes. They led me up through the tea plantation yelling "Shortcut!", before running up less travelled paths.

The tea lay in bushy rows, branches thick with waxy green leaves. My mind recalled a scene from a television show I had seen once on the life of the King Cobra. I imagined snakes sliding with stealth beneath the bushes of tea and regretted having worn my sandals.

The plantations gave way to pine groves which stretched up to a ridge covered in cloud. At the top of the ridge the temperature dropped and the clouds cleared to reveal the centre.

A Singhalese caretaker showed me to a small office where I was introduced to a middle aged German, Michel. His manner was calm, gentle. He noted my passport details in a logbook then handed me a pile of blankets and led me to a small, single room cabin. The view was the mountainous valleys I'd traversed in arriving. There was no electricity, but a basket of candles.

Michel never questioned my reasons for coming and spoke little about the course. He drew my attention to a programme pinned to the back of the door and left me to settle in. It looked extensive, a wake up gong at 4:45am, an itemised day of multiple meditation sessions, breathing workshops and yoga. There were two meals and a light supper in the evening. The day's agenda finished at 9pm. Half an hour a day was devoted to speaking, in a session referred to as 'developing right speech,' conducted in conjunction with an evening tea break. Otherwise, talking was not condoned.

Leaving the room to wash, I noticed a trail of blood from my calf to my foot and, on the stone floor, the engorged body of a leech which I'd evidently collected on my way up.

I fell into the routine. My legs ached from hours spent in the lotus position and my mind rolled, like a video screen set to fast-forward. Crazy scenes raced through my head. The food was basic, vegetarian, sometimes tasty, mostly bland, but the cook served it with a smile. The group numbered twenty and seemed an international mix, but I never really got to know them.

As the days passed I couldn't help but wonder about the lives sitting upright, in silence, beside me. But for only half an hour a day did I hear them speak. I noted talk of beaches, of sunsets, of storms. Talk of love, of lust and death. Talk of music, good food and talk of loved ones missed. But after the telling, nobody dwelt. Reflections were short lived, nothing was held.

On one of the rare days I chose to speak I discussed the best procedure for removing a leech with a young Swedish guy,

"Once attached, leave it to draw its fill, then let it drop off of its own accord…Why not?" he laughed. "It is hungry too and only takes what it can, which is much less than you have to give."

After the first week had passed I realised I much preferred to listen rather than talk. The voice of another, after a day of silence, became increasingly like music to my ears. There was no time for idle banter. Those who choose to speak did so in a concise way. Whether it had something to do with the time in between, the hours spent not talking, or their life a world away became, somehow, inconsequential.

At night, as I made my way back to my room, fireflies covered the darkened sky like low lying stars. I was exhausted yet more conscious of the way I walked. I was beginning to feel more aware of the way I ate, the way I drank. So much more becomes apparent when you cannot escape yourself by talking.

Restlessness was my foe, attacking my concentration, infiltrating my austerity. My conscience, like the sole viewer at my very own picture show, sought an explanation for all the madness, misconduct, joy and adventure I had experienced as it rolled through my mind. I pined for nothingness. I could not fight for it, that much I understood, and as delusions ran rampant in my head I knew I would be a fool to chase them, that much I was beginning to understand.

Then one evening towards the end of my stay I walked into a forest at the back of the centre. I passed through thick undergrowth, broad trunks, tangles of grass and shrubs laden with iridescent flowers, until eventually I emerged at a cliff which dropped to a series of far reaching valleys.

I walked out onto a rocky outcrop, a natural stone platform, which looked down upon an extensive geographic system stretching wide below. Villages sprouted out of twisted hills lushly coated in green. All was illuminated by soft shafts of light from a sky patched with a maze of broken cloud. I looked up willing my eyes to ingest it all. Faint scraps of blue, so small and distant, filtered through, beacons, of sorts, so far away, unobtainable. I felt heavy with the sum of my life so far, all my hopes and aspirations, all the joy, all the heartache, all the unachieved, unfulfilled and neglected. All of which had weighed me down. I needed to offload, then, all of a sudden, I felt it all go.

The walk through the thicket of woods represented my life in its entirety. The hill I had just traversed was the distance I'd come, that I'd lived. While the far-flung beacon of blue represented the challenge of all there was yet to come, only a hole in the cloud through which the sun shone. There were no great claps of thunder, no booming voice raining down from above, but there was an incredible sense of peace and as I looked down and out onto the rolling green valley in before me, I felt something deep inside of me suddenly give. There was a sense of freedom as I struggled to understand what it all meant and caught in my hand the first of many tears which ran down my cheek.

Curry

I left Nilambe in the clouds; thick condensation had again enveloped the centre's grounds. A simple breakfast of dahl and naan bread sat in my stomach. I walked down through the fields of tea, stopping to take photos of the Tamil women at work - big smiles, sorry teeth. I found a leech on my forearm and let it drink its fill. For twenty minutes it held till it fell, bouncing onto the track, full, fat, content. I watched it drag itself off the dirt and into the grass. Behind me the last three weeks had been swallowed up, enveloped by the cloud, a dream? My mind, though a long way from enlightened, was also content. I waited by the roadside for a bus back to Kandy.

A rich cloud of exhaust. The bus was crowded. I squeezed into the front alongside the driver and his companion who was wearing a fez. The banter of the bus rang out in direct contrast to all I had become accustomed to. As it raced down the narrow mountain road my attentions were drawn to a bunch of spring-loaded plastic flowers dancing on the dashboard.

I ate my lunch in an old bake-house in the centre of the city where musty carpets lined the floors. Two monks sat nearby eating cream cakes. Their robes matched the drab maroon curtains which hung across the windows and all but one wall, covered instead in a stained and peeling wallpaper scene, a pictorial, a naff alpine setting, snow-capped mountains towering over a sparkling lake, a golden oak tree indomitable in a grassy foreground.

The restaurant's radio was tuned to the local radio station, "Gold FM 93.5, island wide," announced by a deep, cheesy DJ voice, before Olivia Newton John's 'Hopelessly Devoted' played out loud. A lonesome balding businessman, wearing a fake gold watch, pushed curry into rice, methodically, with his right hand. A group of women in bright saris laughed over tea to Stevie Wonder's 'Happy-Birthday' while waiters in high buttoned shirts and wide bow ties served people, smiling to UB40's 'Keep on Moving.' The waiter assigned to me placed my dishes and threw me an almost sinister grin.

"Do you like hot curry, sir?"

Light flashed off his teeth. He had good teeth, almost perfect teeth.

"Yes, thank you," I replied. "It makes me feel alive."

The sweat rolled from my forehead. The curry burned me deep inside. It was pleasure and it was pain. In my mind, eight thousand kilometres away, a girl, she was still there, hadn't gone anywhere. The waiter reappeared to collect my empty plates.

"And perhaps Sir will have some dessert?"

"Sure, what do you suggest?"

"Ah Sir, today you are very lucky, for we have something very special, fruits of the season: banana custard and mangosteen ice cream."

"Hah, sure," I laughed. "I would love some."

I left the restaurant and walked back to the guesthouse. The chilli in the curry had enticed endorphins from deep within and adrenaline surged through my body. I felt at ease yet sensed restlessness lurking, waiting to destroy my newfound composure, waiting to invade my head space. Restlessness, indecisiveness, thoughts of love… gone.

Jomson was nowhere to be seen. I made myself comfortable in a room and spent the evening alone, drinking tea in the courtyard surrounded by laundered monk robes. The rhythmic flapping of the fabric echoed in my head helping to keep the restlessness at bay.

What do I want from a perfect island anyway? Jomson's profundity, thoughts of his island, washed over me. What do I see when faced with utopia? Is it space I seek? Where do I belong? Where is my tropical island?

I realised I was a long way from the innocence I once had. Of course some people are deemed better at losing their innocence than others, some people are damned good at it. But we all succumb, eventually, no matter how perfect, moralistic or perceptive we happen to be, we all succumb. My brief foray into meditation had left me feeling clear, clean, with a sense of space.

Is space the tropical island I had sought? Is that where my lost innocence lies, waiting to be regained?

I laid my head down on the hard mattress of a monk's bed. Tomorrow would be another day. I would pack my bag, bid the city called Kandy goodbye, and walk away.